You could'ner make it up!

(The 25 post-Waddington Stoke City managers that led to the Premier League!)

Compiled by D Lee

LBA books

First published in Great Britain in 2008 by

LBA books
c/o www.impossibledreamers.co.uk
Stoke-on-Trent

Copyright © 2008 D Lee

A CIP catalogue record for this book is available from the British Library

ISBN 978-0-9541-2144-0

Printed in Stoke-on-Trent by Wood Mitchell

Introduction (the bit we couldn't make up)

It is 1977, and the world is changing.

Things on the way out include hippy pop music, Labour and the Trade Unions, Mike Yarwood, Elvis Presley and naff science-fiction films.

Things coming in include Punk Rock, Margaret Thatcher, Star Wars, ... and relegation for Stoke City FC from the First Division (in the days when First meant Top).

Now, I'm certainly not implying that the Stoke manager should have put a safety pin through his nose, thwacked his players with a handbag, and given a pre-match team talk involving the phrase "May The Force Be With You!" Somehow I don't think it would have made any difference to the state of things, although his life insurance might have been invalidated in some way.

But after almost 17 years, with the club several weeks away from relegation, Tony Waddington stepped down as Stoke boss in March 1977. The era was ended, and the error was about to begin.

But what's a little relegation from the top flight to worry about, particularly when you're amongst friends? When Man Utd got relegated in 1974, they bounced straight back. When Spurs got relegated in 1977, they bounced straight back. And when Burnley got relegated in 1976....(er, yes, I'll get back to you on them later).

Take it from me, this man was a God!
(© Bob Bond)

As for Tony Waddington, or "Wad The God", as he could often be referred to (that's "Wad" rhyming with "God", you understand; not with "Bad", as that wouldn't make any sense at all), well, Tony transformed a mediocre Second Division club into exciting First Division regulars.

Peter Dobing – sadly not even mentioned <u>once</u> in this book.
(© Bob Bond)

Mind you, it took him 3 seasons to get promotion, which isn't so bad really, although with that form today he wouldn't have lasted till Christmas. Overall, he also lost more games as Stoke manager than he actually won, so maybe today they'd have replaced him by Bonfire Night. And then the average attendances in his first season (1960/61) fell dramatically to a 50 year low, so it's amazing he lasted to the end of the school holidays. In fact, given that in his first season Stoke finished 18th, a place lower than the previous season, it's a miracle he got past the pre-season friendlies.

But after promotion to the First Division in 1963, there was no looking back. 14 consecutive seasons of the hurly burly of exciting new players, rubbing shoulders with the Uniteds, the Hotspurs and Burnley (oh, not THEM again). And those FA Cup games, particularly the semi-finals against the lucky lucky Arsenal (& their Goodison programme seller).

But, of course, apart from the 17 years in charge, promotion to enjoy 14 seasons in the top flight, bringing Stanley Matthews back to Stoke, those Arsenal semi-finals, the almost winning the league championship, the qualifying for Europe & almost beating Ajax, and the signing of Alan Hudson (who never lets us forget it, either),....what has this Waddington guy ever done for us Stoke fans? Oh yes, of course, he built the side that beat Chelsea to win the 1972 League Cup Wembley final. Okay, fair enough.

And that's the problem. All this does is mark Tony Waddington as "the guy who just can't be followed". And, boy, have they tried.

But this isn't Tony Waddington's story. No, this is the story of the 25 good-men-and-true, who followed him. Actually, I'm not sure how good-and-true they really were. I mean, we are talking about the likes of Alan Ball and Joe Jordan.

This is the story of a comedy of errors, a string of injustices; a catalogue of mistakes made over & over again, with defeats snatched from the jaws of victories, of disasters waiting to happen, of Titanics waiting to hit ice-bergs, of metaphors and clichés rolling on for paragraph after paragraph....

...until you realise that what this book is really about is the 25 post-Waddington managers of Stoke City, doomed to forever live in the wake of the great man until promotion to the Premier League is finally achieved. Bit like all those ghosts in that last Lord Of The Rings film. But only a bit like them.

Tony Waddington

The modest man himself!
(©Philip Neill)

And anyone who thinks that these guys aren't deserving of a book all to themselves and their achievements, consider this sobering thought: In the 100 years before Tony Waddington there had been just 15 Stoke managers. In the 29 years following him there were 25 managers. Even Burnley haven't had that many.

And, if you're really giving this any great thought, you may say that it's unfair to call them something inane like the 25 men of the Stoke Wilderness Years, but I'm going to call them that anyway. So, tough luck.

Right, let's make a start! First up are Waddo's right-hand men, George Eastham and Alan A'Court (see below).

Alan A'Court long before he joined Tony Waddington's coaching staff in 1969

A Brief Note From The Authors:

This book is based on the many discussions, emails and text-messages exchanged by the authors over many years. Check out the Appendix at the back, which gives the season-by-season divisional positions. It won't help much, but it does include the smallest joke in history. Thank you.

No.1 - George Eastham

22 March 1977 – 9th January 1978

Where did he come from? Stoke hero of the 1972 League Cup Final, where he scored the winner. You must have heard about it. It was in all the papers.

Just one goal? Surely there's another reason for him to become Stoke manager? Well, he had been coaching for years, particularly for the "Cape Town Spurs".

Was it kosher to be coaching in South Africa in the 1970s? Only if you've scored the winner in the 1972 League Cup Final, it seems. It gives you worldwide god-like status (well, in Stoke it does), but more on that later.

Any actual experience of coaching in the UK? Sure, when he hung up his boots in 1975, he became Tony Waddington's assistant manager.

Carefree George Eastham before the burden of management

And this was a success? Er, not particularly. Stoke moved from being Championship contenders (5th - 1974, 5th - 1975) to relegation favourites (12th - 1976, 21st - 1977). Mind you, some people blame it all on an Act Of God; or rather a freak wind that blew the roof off the Butler Street Stand, thus causing a financial crisis, thus the sale of players, thus the loss of form, thus etc etc...

So it was always going to end in tears? Well, under George Stoke got relegated from the First Division, if you mean that. And then they did a "Burnley".

Doing a "Burnley"? Yeah, failed to bounce straight back. And let's face it, after 30 years Burnley are still looking for their bounce.

How on earth did Stoke get relegated? By losing the last two games of the **1976/77** season to WBA (1-3) and Aston Villa (0-1). These two final games were played two days apart, and one win or two draws would have saved

George Eastham

George at Wembley
(©Philip Neill)

Stoke from relegation. Bewilderingly, Stoke weren't anywhere near the relegation zone all season, even when they parted company with Tony Waddington, and only dropped into the relegation zone for the first time after the WBA game. The Villa game was settled by a highly controversial penalty.

His high point as manager?
Managing a First Division club. However, he only won one First Division game though, albeit against Leeds United, out of his 13 games as a First Division manager.

His low point as manager? Managing a Second Division club. After First Division football, here were Stoke losing to the likes of Mansfield Town (1-2), Notts County (0-2), Orient (0-2), and even Burnley (0-1)! Home form was good, but away form was appalling. Eastham was then forced to sell star player Peter Shilton to Nottingham Forest. In December 1977 they lost 4 out of 5 games, and went from promotion possibles to plausible relegation candidates.

What was his autobiography called? It was entitled "*Determined to Win*".

Isn't that ironic? Well, yes, it is, although in fairness it was written in 1964 about how he almost single-handedly overturned footballers' contracts concerning transfers - thus creating the football millionaires we have today. He also wrote a coaching book in 1966 called "*Soccer Science - How to Play and Win*". Oh dear, that doesn't make things any better, does it.

Should Stoke have seen this one coming? I'm afraid so. Hiring ex-legends rarely works out. Like Port Vale and Stanley Matthews in the 1960s, when he went through his "Well, I had always been a Port Vale fan" phase, and that ended in tears.

Who was Port Vale's manager whilst all this was going on? Vale also had one of their old heroes as their manager, Roy Sproson. Roy felt he could adequately do his job whilst also running the local newsagent store (strange, but true!). The Vale Board (ultimately) saw things differently.

Best transfer? It was Eastham who signed Howard Kendall for £40,000. Kendall helped get Stoke promoted (eventually).

Little known facts about George Eastham? Despite scoring prolifically for Newcastle and Arsenal (approximately one goal in every four games), he only scored 5 goals in 239 appearances for Stoke (although one was at Wembley against Chelsea, although I think we have covered that already). He was also in the 1966 England World Cup squad, though didn't get a game. He

George in typical footballer pose for his debut book. (courtesy of Random House Group Ltd)

recently auctioned his 1966 red England No.22 shirt. (It failed to reach its £6000 reserve.) And finally, he almost didn't get the Stoke manager's job as ex-Wolves legend Derek Dougan was also supposedly being courted.

Did he get sacked after a bad defeat? Actually no, Stoke had just beaten non-league Tilbury 4-0 in the FA Cup. They were then drawn against Blyth Spartans.

*George in the days when
he could only afford one boot.*

How did the Sentinel report it? EASTMAN SACKED …New signings had failed to revitalise the club's fortunes…. The board couldn't allow things to deteriorate any further…. Eastman had turned to youngsters like Garth Crooks to save Stoke from relegation, reversing Waddington's policy of introducing young players more slowly….

Is he the only Stoke manager with an OBE? As far as we know.

So where did George go next? Emigrated to South Africa to coach black youngsters in the Cape Town townships.

So he was a good guy afterall? Didn't I tell you, he scored the winning goal in the 1972 League Cup Final (etc etc).

*George in that famous
red England shirt.*

*(© News Group
Newspapers)*

No.2 - Alan A'Court

9th January 1978 - 13th February 1978 (Caretaker manager)

Is that his real name? Yes! Sounds somewhat French, but he was actually born on Merseyside. He played outside-left for over a decade for Liverpool, mainly under Bill Shankly. He replaced Tom Finney in the England team for the World Cup of 1958, despite being a Second Division player, and played against Brazil ("We couldn't get the ball off them!").

So is this the right time to mention Blyth Spartans? No, not yet.

So how did he get the job? Well, he had been coach at Stoke for 8 years, and then been George Eastham's assistant manager. Seems it was his turn next.

ALAN A'COURT

LIVERPOOL & ENGLAND

After Blyth Spartans Alan didn't have a leg to stand on

Has he written a book about his life in football? Yes, it's called *"Alan A'Court: My Life in Football"*.

You've just made that up, haven't you? No, it's really available to buy.

Does it mention Blyth Spartans? Can't you just forget that for now?

OK, then is it true he played in Liverpool's first ever European competition game at Anfield? Yes, but he left soon after to join Tranmere. He then teamed up with Tony Waddington in 1969.

Would he really have got the Stoke manager's job permanently? Well, not after Blyth Spartans. Oh, God, you've got *me* talking about them now.

Wouldn't it just help to talk about it? OK, here goes: In February 1978 Stoke met non-league Blyth Spartans from the Northern Premier League in the fourth round of the FA Cup at the Victoria Ground in front of nearly 19,000 supporters. First, Stoke went one down, but then they went 2-1 up. It was in the bag, surely. But two late goals from Blyth, and Stoke were out. And so soon was Alan.

Alan of all people should have seen this one coming! One of the great FA Cup upsets of all time was in 1959 when Liverpool were beaten 1-2 by Worcester City of the Southern League North-West Section (which no one even knew existed!). It's not surprising that this shocker is not mentioned that often at Anfield, but guess who was playing up front for Liverpool that day? None other than Alan A'Court.

More stories about Liverpool, Shankly and playing against Brazil

Is history written by the winners? It is a bit unfair to judge Alan on ONE game, particularly as he made several hundred appearances for Liverpool, played for England in the World Cup Finals against Brazil (0-0), Austria (2-2) & the USSR (0-1), as well as coaching the classic Stoke squad that won the League Cup etc.

At least he didn't lose his first game to Burnley! Unfortunately, he lost his first game as caretaker manager to Burnley by 0-1. Then there was a three week break in the season due to snow.

Are you telling me he was manager for five weeks, during which Stoke only played two games, and lost both of them? I know, it doesn't look good on paper: played 2, lost 2. But you have to focus on the positives.

Least likely (fictional) sentence from *"Alan A'Court: My Life in Football"*? "I can't quite put my finger on why I didn't get the Stoke job permanently."

Last sighting? Believed to have given up football and become a newsagent. Well, you can't do both.

No.3 - Alan Durban

13th February 1978 – 11th June 1981

Is he a hero or a zero? Oh, he's a hero, surely, although very few remember him with great affection. Despite one blot on his copybook, he's got to be one of the best of the 25 post-Waddington managers, rivalling Macari and Pulis.

How did he get the job? As a player he won the League Championship with Brian Clough's Derby County, and was a regular for Wales. Taking up management from where Clough left off, he brought his coaching and disciplinary skills to Shrewsbury Town in 1974. He got them promoted back to the Third Division at the first attempt. They were champions the season after he left.

Wasn't he being pursued by Orient? Yes, but he wisely turned them down to join the Potters. Showed he had a bit of sense.

Was there anyone else in the frame? Yes, former Wolves legend, Bill McGarry, but he was busy getting Newcastle relegated.

A typically unflattering photo of Durban

What was it like at Stoke when Durban arrived? Pretty dismal. Stoke were only five points off a relegation trip to the Third Division, they'd just been knocked out of the FA Cup at home to non-league Blyth Spartans and attendances were down by nearly a third. So, fairly normal really. Or at least very much what Stoke fans were to get so used to in the 1990s!

But Mr Durban wasn't having any of that? No, sir! After his first game in charge, a 0-0 home draw with Bolton, Stoke were only THREE points off a relegation place, which *really* made people nervous. However, with eight wins from the next 16 games, Stoke finished a miraculous seventh in the Second Division....

...well clear of relegation...? ....but bizarrely STILL only five points clear of relegation! It was a very tight division, what can I say.

Speedy Alan Durban   (© Philip Neill)

Was 1978/79 any better? This was a cracking season, with Stoke rarely out of the top 2, which was as tight at the top as ... well, something really really tight.

What was the word? The word was consistency: five wins out of six to start with, with a rare defeat finally coming in October. They fought off the likes of Newcastle, West Ham and Bristol Rovers (featuring Tony Pulis). In the new year Stoke only lost two league games, but the second of these was at home to bottom club Blackburn (1-2). It sent them briefly out of the top three, but they followed that by finishing the season with 5 wins in 8 games.

How had they stopped leaking goals? With Mike Doyle (from Manchester City) and Denis Smith in defence they only conceded 31 goals (although that was seven more than champions Crystal Palace) and achieved 21 clean sheets (out of 42 league games).

Did it go to the last game? Yes, Stoke won theirs 1-0 at Notts County, with a late winner by Paul Richardson, and were promoted in third place, a point above Sunderland (one of the few teams to beat Stoke that season).

So, what happened next? Now back in the First Division, Stoke started the **1979/80** season sprightly by beating Coventry and Spurs. Nine games without a win followed, and they spent the rest of the season struggled to stay in the First Division. After beating Aston Villa 2-0 at Easter, they seemed safe, but it was followed by 5 defeats in 6 games, losing to Liverpool twice. 1-0 wins against Brighton and West Brom saw them finishing 18th. It didn't help that they were knocked out of the FA Cup at the first hurdle.

No, it couldn't be possibly be....? Yes, it was Burnley. Bloody Burnley. Here was Stoke back in the First Division being beaten 1-0 by a club about to be relegated to the Third Division. Beggar's belief.

Never mind that. He had got Stoke City promoted to the old First Division in his first full season as manager?! Is there a statue of Alan Durban anywhere to be seen in the city?!?! No.

Was it something he said? You can say that again.

Was it something he said? Yes! After losing their first three away games of the **1980/81** season by 1-5, 0-5 and 0-3, he had the nerve to field a 5-4-1 defensive line-up away to Arsenal. It was working too, up until Stoke conceded two late goals. When he was criticized for this at the subsequent press conference, he snapped "If you want entertainment, go and watch a bunch of clowns!"

Durban ecstatic after a goalless draw with WBA

Oh, he didn't, did he?! I bet that went down well? The press knocked him for it, and supporters judged him on it, describing Durban's usual tactics as a "dour style of play". All for playing 5-4-1 at Highbury. What a cheek!

But loads of teams play 5-4-1 today, don't they? Even the England team have played it. Nick Hornby in Fever Pitch reckons Durban had a point. And The Guardian recently commented on Durban's clowns saying that with such high stakes these days, many managers are tempted down the defensive road, as "enough teams have been relegated wearing caps and bells". Bit ponsy, but you get the drift.

Did it get better? Yes, had a reasonable second season, finishing a respectable 11th (**1980/81**). It was achieved with 18 draws – only 2 other league clubs got more. However, Stoke failed to beat any major teams, and the highlight of the season was doing the double over Leeds United. Attendances were falling back alarmingly to an approximate average of 15,000 from the previous season's 20,000. But Stoke were back where they belonged!

And did Durban build on this platform? No, he quit to join Sunderland.

And his famous parting line? "I wish to manage a big club."

*Alan Durban looking for
a big club to manage*

Ooooohh! That's not nice. Was Sunderland such a great move? Not really. He lasted there till early 1984, and never finished above Stoke. He then took over Cardiff for two seasons, relegated in both. That was affectively it – he'd peaked at Stoke and hadn't realised it.

How did The Sentinel cover his final days? Durban's contract about to expire… Linked with WBA vacancy after Ron Atkinson leaves for Manchester United…Durban unlikely to uproot his family for a move to the north-east…With his achievements he can leave with a clear conscience…

Best transfer? Brendon O'Callaghan springs to mind. Cost £40,000 from Doncaster, and was Durban's first signing. His second signing was for a reserve goalie called Peter Fox (£15,000). Also signed Paul MaGuire from Shrewsbury for £262,000 in 1980. Sold Garth Crooks to Spurs for £650,000 in 1980 – apparently they had a rather heated relationship.

Anything else we should know about Durban? Although renowned for being a track-suit manager himself, he made Howard Kendall his chief coach. Some say the successful 1978/79 season was due to this powerful partnership. But then Kendall left in 1979 for a successful management career of his own, and things at Stoke were never quite the same.

Unlikely name for a Durban autobiography? *"Don't Quote Me On That!"*

No.4 - Richie Barker

24th June 1981 - 9th December 1983

Should you take the advice of an outgoing manager? Not always. Alan Durban recommended Richie Barker to succeed him, but only after failing to persuade Barker to join him at Sunderland.

Wasn't he a pretty obscure choice? Blimey, if you think he's obscure, you just wait!

How did Durban know him? They'd both played at Derby under Brian Clough in the 1960s when Barker was a centre forward. In 1974 he became Durban's assistant at Shrewsbury.

Was this the last time they worked together? Durban desperately wanted Barker to join him at Stoke too when Durban switched clubs in 1978, but Barker stayed to manage the Shrews. The stay only lasted 10 months

Durban and Barker – not as close as you would think.

though, but Barker did leave them on course to win the Third Division Championship. He switched to the then high-flying top-flight Wolves to become assistant manager. One of his first tasks was to mastermind the defeat of Shrewsbury in the FA Cup 6th round. Wolves then won the League Cup in 1980.

So he was a "mover and shaker"? Er, yes. He'd actually been running Wolves for some time, as the then manager John Barnwell was recovering from a serious car accident.

Was he a disaster at Stoke? Certainly not. Two and a half seasons in the top flight. It's hard to knock it.

C'mon, it wasn't that easy!? Started the **1981/82** season well with a 1-0 away win at (ironically) Arsenal, but soon started to struggle. Things then went seriously pear-shaped (a la George Eastham) in March 1982.

Did they lose nine games in a row, by any chance? Nearly. They lost eight games out of nine. In the middle of that they managed a 0-0 home draw…with the mighty Brighton. They then beat Barker's old team Wolves, sending them

down. And just like at the end of George Eastham's season, they had Villa and WBA to play. This time they were both at home, but this time they needed to win both games.

And did they? Yes, 1-0 and 3-0, saved from relegation on the last game. They finished 18th.

One place above Durban's Sunderland? It could be argued that Stoke's win against Wolves saved Sunderland from going down, but that's a bit tenuous and me just being bitchy. (It was more likely the away draw at Leeds!)

He wasn't scared to break Stoke's transfer records? In 1982 he sold Adrian Heath (£700,000) and Lee Chapman (£500,000), but bought Sammy McIlroy (£350,000) winger Mark Chamberlain (£135,000), and Mickey Thomas (£200,000).

In his youth Barker was a happy well-groomed lad.

That must have been some team to watch? Sure was. The **1982/83** season kicked off with another win over Arsenal, 2-1 at home. This time the season didn't fall away, and they spent most of time playing attractive football and vying for a place in Europe, even beating Manchester United 1-0. Pre-Christmas was a bit ropey, losing 5 out of 6 games. However, despite losing 0-4 to his old club Notts County, post-Christmas saw Stoke make steady progress up the league.

Did they invade Europe? No, they didn't win any of their last six games, dropping from 5th to 13th! It was a major disappointment.

It was the beginning of the end? With only two wins in their first 16 league games of **1983/84**, and the attractive football turning into long-ball (a system that he described as "The Attacking Policy"), he lost the player's confidence. Nonetheless, he switched systems to what he called The Defensive System, but that didn't work either, and was pretty grim to watch.

Was there loyalty and unity behind those closed doors?! Hardly. Mickey Thomas and Sammy McIlroy, amongst others, put in transfer requests. The board turned these down, deciding at the meeting to sack Barker instead, despite the fact that he'd just signed a new 18 month contract the previous month.

Where did they suddenly get that idea from? Perhaps from the fact that Vale had just sacked their manager 3 days before.

How did The Sentinel cover it? "Stoke City axe Richie Barker. News broken on wife's birthday!" "Horton tipped as successor to McGrath." (It was actually John Rudge who got the job.)

Richie Barker's parting comment? "I should have stuck to the Attacking Policy." !

Best remembered for? Not being Alan Durban, I suppose.

Barker was either incredibly tall or just used to play in tiny stadiums

No.5 - Bill Asprey

9ᵗʰ December 1983 – 15ᵗʰ April 1985

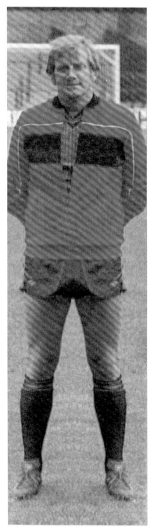

Bill Asprey, when shorts were … short

Was he a hero or a villain? Oh dear. He went from one extreme to the other. In his first season (**1983/84**) he miraculously saved Stoke from relegation from the top flight First Division. Second season was a disaster though.

Who did he think he was? He had been Richie Barker's assistant manager since 1981. Before that he had managed Oxford United. A long time before that, he had played 341 games for Stoke, mainly under Tony Waddington.

Was he the obvious choice? The board were considering Denis Smith, then manager at York, or even Jack Charlton.

Did he *really* save Stoke from relegation in a "miraculous" way? Well, yes and no. When Barker left, Stoke had only 2 wins in 16 games, but were only one point away from safety. After eight games under Asprey, it was 3 wins from 24 games, and 8 points adrift.

So he dug the hole a bit bigger? Sure did. But then he won 10 of the last 18 games, including beating Arsenal (1-0), Aston Villa (1-0) and Liverpool (2-0). Saved on the last day by Paul Maguire hitting all four in a 4-0 win against Wolves, sending them down (again).

Er, weren't Wolves already relegated by this time? Er, yes, actually they were, but you gotta laugh, haven't you.

What was Asprey's secret? Bringing Alan Hudson back from Arsenal. Inspired.

5 - 1

What was Asprey's downfall? Keeping Alan Hudson, probably. For the **1984/85** season the aging midfielder, along with Sammy McIlroy, were getting a bit long in the tooth, and they found themselves surrounded by the former youth team. Hudson soon got injured and when he returned got himself sent off.

What was it like to watch? Painful. On the pitch it was a farce, with neither the defence nor attack having a clue what they should be doing. They went out of the League Cup to Third Division Rotherham, losing at home 1-2. Their top scorer in the league for the whole season was Ian Painter with six goals, and four of them were penalties. By Christmas they only had eight points, but chose Boxing Day to beat Manchester United 2-1 (including a Painter penalty).

Did that spur on a comeback? In the New Year things just got worse, until Easter brought a third (and final) league win, against Arsenal 2-0 (including another Painter penalty). But it was followed by 10 straight defeats to end the season with a record low of 17 points – not worth crossing the street for really.

Bill Asprey looking older than he did when he managed the club!

That's with three points for a win? Yes, it's tenuous as to whether 17 points was really a record low, as Newton Heath got only 14 points in Division 1 if you go back to 1893/94. But that was with only two points for a win, and they did play only 30 matches. But…well, it was pretty bad, anyway.

So they finally got into the record books? Yes, for lowest number of points (17), fewest away goals scored (6), most goals conceded (91), worst goal difference (-67), worst performance by a club in the Football League ever, dropped off the bottom of the pools coupon…oh, you get the idea.

How did Asprey take it? Badly. He'd suffered ill-health just after Christmas, and youth coach Tony Lacey had taken over briefly. The manager blamed the board and the board blamed the manager. The club were already short of cash, and attendances were plummeting to around 10,000. With his health poor (compounded, supposedly, by depression) the club "suspended him from duties" in April 1985. "I have not been allowed to manage," he said; whilst Denis Smith (former Stoke hero), when asked about taking over, was quoted as saying: "I've no wish to commit suicide at the moment." Charming.

So he ended up tarnishing his Stoke legacy? Don't they always? Stoke won only 14 of the 67 games he was in charge for.

And the good news? In that time Stoke beat Liverpool, Manchester United and Arsenal (twice!). More than Alan Durban ever managed.

Improbable line from any forthcoming autobiography? "17 points doesn't sound like many, but it was a damn site more than Derby got last season in the Premier."

STOKE CITY

No.6 - Tony Lacey

15th April 1985 – 24th June 1985 (caretaker)

Was it turning into a Biblical epic? And so it was written, verily, that Alan Durban would begat Richie Barker, who begat Bill Asprey, who begat Tony Lacey. And the Lord looked down at his handiwork and he….

What are you on about? What I mean is that Barker had worked for Durban, Asprey had worked for Barker, and Lacey had worked for Asprey.

And Tony Lacey was the last in the line? Yeah, after him the boot room was empty. As it was, Asprey had been acting coach as well as Manager. Lacey was youth team coach. After him came the ball-boys.

What did he believe in? "I believe in discipline and hard work. We have to roll up our sleeves!"

Is this the same Tony Lacey who played for Port Vale? Ah, I was wondering when you were going to bring that up. He did actually start his playing career at Stoke, but they soon sold him to Vale where he made over 200 appearances. Returned to Stoke as youth coach in the late 1970s.

Can we hold him responsible for Garth Crooks? I'm afraid so. He would also like Lee Chapman and Adrian Heath to be taken into consideration. The players he produced through the youth scheme probably saved Stoke from oblivion, particularly when they couldn't afford to buy anyone.

Port Vale's very own Tony Lacey! He was a tough old boot!

Can we talk about his management career? Er, are you sure you want to do this? You'll need a strong stomach.

C'mon, it can't be all bad? Well, he'd held the reigns briefly in Asprey's absence on New Year's Day for the Coventry game. Got flattened 0-4. Then took over when Asprey was sacked in April 1985. Lost his first game to Everton (0-2), dooming club to relegation (although it was inevitable at this stage). Then set about losing the last seven games as well.

So he is officially Stoke's worst manager? 'Fraid so. Played 8, lost 8. Goals-for 4, Goals-against 20. Over a whole season that would be …. 21-for and 105-against. That's, er, not so good.

Eight defeats had little affect on Tony

But he was the last man standing? Even the Chairman, Frank Edwards, dropped down dead in June, leaving Lacey in charge for a few more weeks than he expected.

Does he get a statue? No, he got to carry on his success as youth team coach, staying on till 1996.

Unlikely entry from Tony Lacey's diary? "Friday 19th April 1985. At last I am the boss!!! My time has come at last!!! Home game against Everton tomorrow. I know my boys will pull it together, and the phoenix will rise from the grave!!! Then we will take over the world!!!"

No.7 - Mick Mills

24th June 1985 – 7th November 1989

A new dawn? Yes, a new dawn of mediocrity.

Mick Mills is best remember for? Barely being remembered at all, despite being in charge for 4 ½ years. Out of 42 applicants (!), he was short listed with John Toshack, although Denis Smith was also still being considered.

But Mick arrived with a lot of promise? He was a former England captain and Ipswich FA Cup winner, but with no management experience.

Did that matter? No, as he'd just completed a 2 week football management course at St Helens the week before. What a bit of luck! (you'd think).

What else did he arrive with? As a Player Manager he was also able to fill the vacant (and vulnerable) left-back position.

Mick Mills – he's no mug…oh, sorry, yes he might be!
(© popartgallery on eBay!)

Anything else? He brought fitness freak and former Wolves manager, Sammy Chung as his coach.

Did it start well? Lost first game of **1985/86** at home to Sheffield United (1-3), then started battling relegation. Then Stoke's England international Mark Chamberlain was snapped up by Sheffield Wednesday for a bargain

£300,000 (set by a miserly tribunal). Then lost 0-3 to bottom club Carlisle United. Then attendances dropped to an average of just 8,288, the lowest for nearly a century. Then…

So it didn't start very well, then? Pulled themselves together up to a point - after going out of the cup to Third Division Notts County - to eventually finish 10th. Beat Leeds United 6-2, although Leeds later beat Stoke 0-4 in the return game.

Mick Mills has an MBE, you know? Er, yes. Then in the next season…

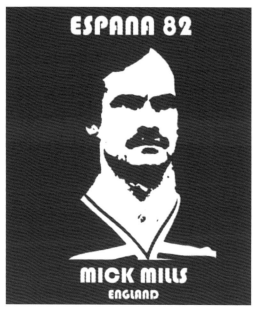

Mick Mills…or a South American dictator?

Wasn't he awarded it in 1984, before he'd joined Stoke? Er, possibly. For services to football, I believe, but…

Not an OBE, like George Eastham? Er, no. Anyway, they started the season….

Do you think it helped him? The MBE? Not at the start of the **1986/87** season, it didn't. They lost 7 of their first 10 games, ending up bottom of the league for most of October, even beaten by Brighton, who went on to finish bottom themselves.

Another bad start that improves later? Mills shored up the defence that by now featured the legendary keeper Peter Fox, Lee Dixon (Mills signed him from Bury), Steve Bould, and captain George Berry. He then brought in old Ipswich mate, Brian Talbot to firm up the midfield. The inspired run that followed had them peaking at 4th place in February, before losing half their remaining games to finish 8th.

Did they beat Leeds United again? Unbelievably, they beat them 7-2 this time. Even put 5 past Sheffield United and Grimsby. This was Mills' finest hour. So much so that Ipswich wanted talks with him, and he upset supporters by claiming to be disappointed not to be allowed to talk with them.

But can we agree that Mick Mills was the dullest of managers? Well, with the little money he had he often bought cheap, average, and often injury-prone players. He soon sold Lee Dixon and Steve Bould to Arsenal, whilst Tony Kelly and later Brian Talbot left for West Brom. Subsequently the **1987/88** season was spent entirely in mid-table, finishing an uninspiring 11th.

Highlight of the season?
Almost beating eventual First Division champions Liverpool in the FA Cup (losing the replay 0-1 at Anfield after a sticky 0-0 draw at the Victoria Ground). This was the season that even die-hards realised that Mick Mills wasn't going to cut it; as such attendances were grim.

And Leeds United? Yes, they beat Leeds again, 2-1 this time, but they had to wait till injury time before George Berry heading home the winner.

After three seasons of mediocrity, surely Mills was for the chop? He just wasn't bad enough to sack. And he kept beating Leeds United. What could the board do? Let him have one more go for the **1988/89** season, then that would be it, surely.

Mick Mills – a future England Captain

Don't tell me, they started the season badly, had a good run in the middle, then fell away at the end? How did you guess? Despite Mills actually signing someone half-decent for a change (Peter Beagrie) and some ruffian called Chris Kamara, Stoke didn't win a game till the end of September. They then got beat by Fourth Division Orient in the League Cup. They finally got it together to reach 7th place mid-season. And then, same old story, 8 defeats and one victory in their last 14 games, ending 13th.

Any highlights? Losing 0-4 to Leeds, 1-5 to Ipswich, 0-4 to Plymouth, and, best of all, 0-6 to West Brom. All thankfully away from home....

Good thing they didn't lose any embarrassing games at home?! ...and then lost 0-3 at home to bottom club, Walsall, who by then were already relegated.

Mick was a happy-go-lucky young man, waiting patiently to grow a moustache

Just as well Mills' contract had run out, eh?! Ah.

What do you mean "Ah."? Well, four seasons mid-table in the Second Division didn't seem so bad (certainly not later on, it didn't), and anyway, the board clearly couldn't think of anyone else.

Oh, for heaven's sake! Well, at least they didn't give him any money to spend? Ah.

Don't tell me! The board cobbled together £1 million for him to spend. Amongst others he bought Ian Cranson (£450,000 and nearly ready for his second knee operation) and Wayne Biggins (£250,000, and seriously off-form).

At least he didn't have the added pressure of having Port Vale in the same league? Unfortunately, Vale had just got promoted and were in the same league.

So – don't tell me – the 1989-90 season started poorly, as it always did with Mills, then revived in the middle, then drifted off at the end? Well, sort of. Except the start was EXTREMELY poor. Couldn't even beat Vale at home. First win wasn't until mid-October, and it was followed not by a revival, but by four straight defeats, the last of which was a 0-6 hammering by Swindon Town. "I've been in worse positions than this," he said, trying to say something helpful.

Good thing for Mills that he didn't have an assistant manager who was tailor-made to take his place? Unfortunately, Mills had just hired Alan Ball a few weeks before.

Ah. So Mills was sacked. Shame really, as he'd just sold Peter Beagrie to Everton for £750,000, just to compound matters. This meant that over his time at Stoke he had made a transfer profit of £½million.

Overstayed his welcome? Should have found another job a year or two before, and done himself a favour.

But he didn't actually do badly at Stoke, did he? Not at all, but his reign always seemed like a big disappointment.

Another manager who'd peaked at Stoke without realising it? Absolutely. And to prove it, two months later in January 1990 he was put in charge of Fourth Division Colchester United, who were then one place off the bottom spot. He stayed till May, by which time Colchester were firmly rooted to last place, six points adrift, and relegated to the Vauxhall Conference. Only then did he decide to go back to coaching.

Most likely to say in a forthcoming autobiography? "I lasted four and a half years, the longest running manager Stoke have had since Tony Waddington."

Least likely to say in a forthcoming autobiography? "It took me four and half years to lure Alan Ball to Stoke, just so that I could drop him right in it!"

No.8 – Alan Ball

7ᵗʰ November 1989 – 23rd February 1991

Maybe we should miss Alan Ball out? Certainly not.

Yes, but you'll only get upset again? I've calmed down a bit since then. It *is* nearly 20 years ago.

So, Alan Ball becomes manager by default after Mills was dismissed, and ... NOOOOO!!!! WHY HIM?! WASN'T THERE ANYONE ELSE?!?!? OH GOD, I CAN'T TAKE IT!!!

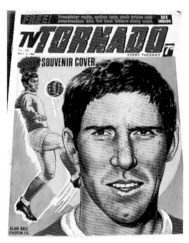

Yes, this really was supposed to be Alan Ball (part 1)

Hiring him was not a great idea then? Not really, no.

A big mistake by the board? After 8 managers in 12 years, what makes you think they were ready to make a mistake?!?

Didn't Alan Ball's World Cup winning medal mean anything to fans? His efforts managing Portsmouth probably meant more. He put Pompey back on the map after years in the doldrums, but he probably peaked there. It was downhill after that. After leaving them, Mills plucked him to help stabilize a sinking ship, before being pushed overboard himself, leaving Ball at the wheel with his feet getting wet.

Good things to say about Alan Ball? He won his first match 3-2 against Brighton, with Carl Beeston scoring in the first minute. He signed Lee Sandford and Noel Blake, both ex-Portsmouth players, and a certain Dave Kevan from Notts County. He salvaged an unlikely point at Port Vale. He made Mick Mills look like a God (although why that's a good thing, I'm not sure). He had a picture of Winston Churchill on his desk. He said things like "We only want players who are ready to die for this club!". He played at Bristol Rovers with Tony Pulis.

So how did he cope with the Titanic? Actually, seeing it was only November when he took over, there was plenty of time to sort things out. They were only two points from safety, and only one point from safety after his debut Brighton game.

Where did it all go wrong? The ever changing team won only 4 remaining games, and lost 14. Defeat after defeat drove the fans mad, even violent, and when Ball criticized them for being so negative, they turned on him. Stoke finished bottom, 13 points from safety, relegated to the Third Division for the first time in over 60 years.

Thank goodness it didn't get any worse? Here they were in **1990/91**, one league below Port Vale, mixing with the likes of Orient, Mansfield, Chester and Exeter, … and losing to them. [It is interesting to note that Birmingham, Bolton, Fulham, Wigan and Reading were also in the same league – curiously, Stoke did actually do better against them!!]

Well, at least they didn't lose to bloody Burnley in the FA Cup? And then they lost 0-2 to bloody Burnley in the FA Cup. (They were in the Fourth Division at the time.)

Any other bad news? The team were crap, the board were too broke to replace them, and the Taylor Report was calling for all-seater stadiums. If that wasn't bad enough for Alan Ball, he was hounded by fans inside and outside the ground.

Yes, this really was supposed to be Alan Ball (part 2)

The final nail in the coffin? After starting relatively well, Stoke dropped into the lower half of the league. With five games without a win, then a 0-4 defeat at Wigan, followed by another demonstration by fans against him, Alan Ball resigned. Stoke had never been as low as 14th in the Third Division, and were floundering, not knowing what to do about it.

Did Ball ever recover? Amazingly he carried on managing. Did a reasonable job at Exeter, who Stoke beat only once (5-2) in 4 meetings. Did well at

Southampton, but unwisely quit them to take over Manchester City, who were relegated from the Premiership in his first and only season.

But wasn't he "relegated with every team he managed"? No, that's just an urban myth. He quit Blackpool and Exeter well before they were relegated, and he skilfully saved Southampton from the drop, taking them to 10th in the Premiership. When he was re-appointed Portsmouth manager in 1998 they were several points adrift at the bottom of the table. He masterminded a miraculous escape that saw two of his former sides (Stoke City and Manchester City) relegated after Pompey won 3-1 at Bradford City on the final day of the season.

An early curiously-titled autobiography
(courtesy of Random House Group Ltd)

Ah, but wasn't he voted 7th in The Guardian's Top 10 Worst Managers Of All Time? Er, yes, that is true, although their suggestion that he told his Manchester City players that they only needed a draw in their last game for survival, when in fact they needed a win, is misleading (although bloody funny). They sum him up as a lovely man, but a lousy manager. Harsh.

Thank goodness he hasn't written a book telling his side of the story. In his book, *Playing Extra Time*, he gets the chance to tell his side of the story.

Oh dear, what does he say? He claims he was happy at Colchester, and only moved to Stoke as his father had coached there under Waddington. He arrived to find despairing Mills and Chung in a "shaky mental state", with supporters jeering them at every opportunity. Mills put Ball in charge of the team almost immediately, but Ball found that the players were chronically demoralised. He admits that it was HIM that sold Beagrie, not Mills, to pay for new players. He says that the board were more interested in rowing about catering contracts than with fighting relegation, and that the backroom staff (with the exception of Tony Lacey and Ron the kit man) were wholly inadequate.

Anything else?! He claims that although he took the blame for Chris Kamara leaving, it was actually Kamara who begged him for a transfer to pay off his insurmountable debts. Ball says he had actually agreed a deal with Middlesbrough, but the board went behind Ball's back to prod Kamara towards Leeds. He hated the supporters doing their conga on the terraces as he saw it as them laughing at the manager. Before that fateful Wigan game, a 10 year old Stoke fan came out of the crowd before the game and spat at Ball. The players then played so "pathetically" that he quit after the match. He says he couldn't get away from Stoke fast enough – well, that's no surprise. There, that's saved you having to buy the book.

Another player with an MBE? Indeed, and only the second 1966 World Cup winner to die. He was only 61. The BBC rather bizarrely wrote "Ball collapsed outside his home after tackling a bonfire". Read into that what you will.

Four world cup heroes... in the Gents?!?

Not in the least bit related to...? Alan Ball, the creator of the TV series, Six Feet Under. Mind you, now you mention it...

No.9 - Graham Paddon

23rd February 1991 – May 1991 (caretaker manager)

Another case of last man standing? Yes, Graham "Budgie" Paddon was assistant manager under Alan Ball. As the board couldn't afford to just hire another manager immediately (they had their eye on Denis Smith again, who was now at Sunderland), they let Budgie flutter on for the rest of the season.

Budgie?! Yes, he used to be known as Budgie at Norwich City as his long blonde hair looked like Adam Faith's 1970s Budgie TV character.

Graham Paddon in the pink!
(© News Group Newspapers)

Where have I heard his name before? Paddon is better known for setting up the second West Ham goal in the 1975 FA Cup final, and scoring the winner in the Cup Winners Cup semi-final in Frankfurt.

Where did he appear from? Was the coach at Portsmouth under Alan Ball, and joined him at Stoke in December 1989.

What was Paddon's role? On both occasions Alan Ball sold the team's best player to pay for a set of new players. Paddon managed to coach the subsequent Portsmouth players out of relegation, but he couldn't produce the same miracle at Stoke – the job was just too insurmountable.

Best remembered for? Genuinely thought of as a nice guy.

Do nice guys come first? Well, as this was Stoke's worst ever season, it's difficult to be objective. He took over with the club 14th in the Third Division. He lost the first game dismally to Bournemouth, with ex-Vale striker Andy Jones taking Stoke's defence apart. That went down badly.

So Stoke could easily have ended up in the Fourth Division?! Paddon wasn't going to allow that. After the Bournemouth game, Stoke played 8 games in 25 days, winning five of them to put the club on the brink of the play-offs.

So why didn't he become Stoke's full time manager? He lost the chance by losing six games in a row (including 1-2 to Lou Macari's Birmingham City). Stoke ended up finishing 14th, which was exactly where Budgie came in.

Most memorable game? Winning 4-0 away to high-flying Brentford. Mind you, it was a bit out of the blue.

Where did he end up? After not getting the Stoke job, he ended up back at Portsmouth as assistant manager to Jim Smith. Later became a football scout.

What does Alan Ball say about him in his autobiography? He describes Paddon as his "old companion" at one point. However,

Don't be afraid, it's merely Budgie the hairy Norwich City player

despite working closely together for some years, Ball barely mentions Paddon at all. Odd.

There's really no excuse for this haircut.

No.10 – Lou Macari

18ᵗʰ June 1991 – 26ᵗʰ October 1993

Oh, lo, the Chosen One appeared through the mist, and verily they all bowed down before him chanting…chanting... "Lou Lou, skip to my Lou, Skip to my Lou Macari!"

What made him think he was the right man for Stoke City? Dunno. He didn't have an OBE, he hadn't won the World Cup or even the League Championship, and he hadn't captained England or won a Fourth Division championship medal (à la Richie Barker). He was also quite an experienced manager already, so he certainly didn't seem like Stoke City management material.

Wasn't he relegated with Manchester United soon after he joined them in 1973? Scoff all you like, at least he has a Second Division championship medal when United went straight back up the following season.

OK, so wasn't it he who scored the winning goal in the 1977 FA Cup final against Liverpool? Yes. A deflected shot off former Stoke star Jimmy Greenhoff, but they all count. It helped him forget losing to Second Division Southampton in the final the previous

Lou Macari, when things were good at Celtic   (©Bob Bond)

season. Before that he'd apparently won countless medals for Celtic in the early 1970s, but – let's face it - who follows Scottish football?! All we know was that he was the smallest player ever to play for Scotland.

Why did he always give the impression of being a loveable rogue?
Apparently when he joined Stoke he was under investigation for non-payment of tax, and was charged for unauthorised betting on a match involving Swindon (whom he was managing at the time). Although he was acquitted years later, fans kind of liked the idea that he was a bit of a rough diamond.

Any luck as a manager? Promoted twice with Swindon, did OK at West Ham, but – and this is the important bit – won the Leyland DAF Cup with Birmingham! Of course, soon afterwards he fell out with their board (as he seemed to do everywhere he went), this time over the "size of the squad".

And so he was snapped up by Stoke? Ah, not immediately. Firstly, Birmingham offered him a 3 year contract and their fans begged him to stay. Then Celtic briefly considered him, and Macari hung on till he failed to make the short-list. Stoke meanwhile couldn't agree an acceptable compensation deal to steal Bournemouth's manager, one Harry Redknapp. Subsequently, after several weeks Stoke and Macari were united!

An old tin badge of Lou Macari.
Yes, he was that famous!

So, did Macari have Stoke playing wild attacking football right from the start of 1991/92?! Not exactly. He bought big Vince Overson to put alongside big Ian Cranson and Lee Sandford to shore up that leaky defence. Waddington, Durban and Pulis - who also made defence their first priority - would have been proud of him. (Waddington's defence was known as "Waddington's Wall".)

So not very attacking at all at first? It wasn't a very winning start, grubbing around in the lower half of the league. But Wayne Biggins suddenly started scoring, Liverpool were almost beaten in the Rumbelow's Cup, and then Macari signed some guy called Mark Stein on loan from Oxford United.

How did the famous Steino start out? Despite failing to score in his five games on loan, Macari risked it and signed Stein permanently. Soon it was a Stein-Biggins goal-fest, with 40 goals between them. Even sooner, Stoke began creeping into play-off territory, and the crowds returned.

What they needed was a good FA Cup run…? Sadly they went out of the FA Cup in the first round.

Thank goodness they didn't lose to one of those embarrassing non-league teams!? Unfortunately they lost to one of those embarrassing non-league teams, Telford United (1-2), whom they had beaten the previous season under Alan Ball.

An early Macari autobiography with all those Celtic medals

At least they beat Macari's old club, Birmingham? They sure did, 2-1, but there was bad blood there and a pitch-invasion during the 1-1 draw at St Andrews. Stoke also knocked Birmingham out of the Autoglass Trophy, but Birmingham had the last laugh as they got automatic promotion. Alan Ball's Exeter were also beaten (5-2), but yobs spat at and abused Ball, who might have been better off not turning up.

Any really good laughs to lighten things up a bit? Sure. Port Vale got relegated. Hell, we're easily pleased.

Why weren't Stoke promoted? Well, they hit the top of the table in February after beating top side WBA 1-0. They were still top in mid-April, but lost their last two games, including a home game to lowly Chester (1-0), to finish 4th, making the playoffs.

Any luck in the playoffs? No, got knocked out by Stockport County (0-1 & 1-1), then managed by the slightly off-side Danny Bergara from Uruguay. Stockport went on to be beaten by Peterborough, who Stoke had beaten to get to Wembley in the Mickey Mouse Cup, or the Autoglass Trophy as it was now called by supporters.

At last, Wembley again!? Yes, and victory again. Revenge is sweet as The Golden One, Mark Stein, scores the only goal of the game to defeat Stockport.

So Macari brought the good times back? Well, they were still in the Third Division if that's what you mean (although in 1992 it changed names to Division Two). But the team played with verve, the goals started to flow again, and they had a manager with charisma at last.

And did this charisma inspire them to greatness? Well, the **1992/93** season started as sluggishly as usual. But then in mid-September Stoke beat top-club WBA in a 4-3 thriller, and results started going their way. Macari followed this by selling opinionated Wayne Biggins to Barnsley, and then suddenly they were motoring. In November they went top of the table and stayed there for the rest of the season, closely chased by Port Vale, who falter at the end and lost in the playoffs (tragically).

And local pride was back? Macari's Stoke did the double over Vale (2-1 and 2-0, with Mark Stein the destroyer!), which ultimately cost their neighbours promotion. Vale's revenge was knocking Stoke out of the Autoglass (0-1) and the FA Cup (1-3, the game where Dave Regis's goal-bound shot got stuck in the Vale Park mud before it could cross the line).

And Macari was innocent! Sure was. Average crowds rose to over 16,500, the highest for a decade, and only bettered in 2008. Stoke finished Champions with 93 points, and Stein with 30 goals. The future looked good, with everything coming together on and off the pitch. The man least-likely had turned things around in style.

That book
(Published by Bantam Press August 2008)

It couldn't last? Of course it couldn't. Unbeknown to fans, the club were seriously in debt, which restricted Macari's transfer manoeuvres for the **1993/94** season.

I hope they beat West Brom? Of course they did, 1-0, but the going was tough in the new First Division.

At least they didn't have to play the likes of Manchester United!?! And then they were drawn against Manchester United, Macari's old side, in the Coca-Cola Cup. Although playing against a makeshift United team, Stoke beat them 2-1 (although they lost the second leg 0-2).

Was this the last great victory for Macari to go out on?! Symbolically, yes, but only because it was more memorable than the 1-0 defeat of Grimsby 10 days later. Celtic and Liverpool had been sniffing around Macari, and when the club was forced to sell Stein to Chelsea, Macari took his dream job at his beloved Celtic.

What if..? Yes, what if the Celtic job hadn't come up? Most people reckon Macari would have used the Stein money to build a new team that would have taken Stoke to the Premier League within 2-3 years.

If only Lou Macari had written a book about his life in football? Macari has recently written a book about his life in football called *Football, My Life*.

Well, there's a bit of luck! What does it say about his time at Stoke? Ah, well, as I write this, it hasn't actually been published yet, so we don't know.

Not held up for legal reasons by any chance?! Ha Ha! Very funny. No, of course not. However, his editor tells me he has some hilarious anecdotes about Nello the Clown (aka my old mate kit-man Neil Baldwin - Ed) and remembers both his stints at Stoke with "great affection".

Best remembered for? Being a God, albeit a little one. He brought football back to the Victoria Ground, so he'll never have to buy a drink in Stoke ever again.

No.11 – Chic Bates

26th October - 10th November 1993 (caretaker manager)

Real name? Phil Bates, or Philip D Bates to be precise.

So why "Chic"? Dunno, maybe he liked the 1970s disco band "Chic".

Yes, anyway; so where did Philip appear from? Well, apart from playing at Bristol Rovers with Tony Pulis, he was another one who was big in Shrewsbury (like Durban & Barker), having played there over 400 times and becoming player-manager in 1984 (they were doing well in the old 2nd Division at the time) till 1987 (when they started not doing so well).

What did he do next? He became a professional stalker.

I beg your pardon?! He started to follow Lou Macari around. Seemed to be stuck to him like glue. First he joined Lou at Swindon, then to Birmingham, then to Stoke. After that it was briefly up to Celtic, back to Stoke again, and then – as Lou was out of management – Phil went back to Shrewsbury. Twice.

Can we do Joe Jordan now? Not yet. We haven't covered Philip's time in charge.

But it was only two weeks!? But what a ride it was! First, Stoke came from 0-2 down to beat Barnsley 5-4. Four days later they beat Sunderland 1-0 with a superb late goal by Orlygsson. Three days after that they muscled their way past Watford by 3-1. The team went from 14th to 8th in 7 days. 100% success rate.

Does that make Chic Bates Stoke's best ever manager? Certainly looks like it. But after failing to get the Stoke job, he rejoined Macari at Celtic.

Bates hiding in the shadows

Unlikely line from his unlikely autobiography? "After three wins in a fortnight, the board should have given me another two weeks, and then we'd have been top of the league!!" (extract from the sadly fictitious "*I Should Never Have Left Shrewsbury Town (Twice)*".)

No.12 – Joe Jordan

10th November 1993 – 8th September 1994

So this is the famous Joe Jordan? Sure is. Winner of the League Championship with Leeds, and veteran of three World Cups with Scotland. He even played in that famous Scotland vs Holland game in 1978. Also, a colleague of Lou Macari's at Manchester United.

Any good in management? He revitalised Bristol City, but after a less successful time at Hearts he ended up assisting Liam Brady for a few weeks at Celtic, who were going through a rough time (ie not winning every game).

How rough did it get? The story goes that when Liam left, Jordan stayed on as caretaker, believing the board might offer him the job, only to quit after only one day when he found that they were looking for a replacement (ie. Lou Macari). So Jordan joined Stoke in return. He beat off Chic Bates and Martin O'Neil for the job.

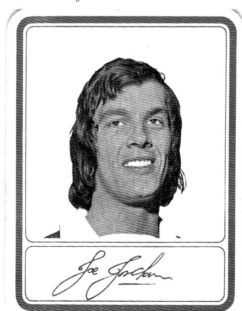

He looked like a God but was later found to be Scottish

Oh, lucky old us! Hey, he wasn't so bad. He started in 8th spot, and won his first game 1-0 against 3rd place Leicester. But after that Stoke failed to beat any of the top sides. After bobbing around the play-off positions for so long, they only managed to draw their last three games, and slumped to finish 10th.

Why was he so unpopular with fans? Trouble was, he had the dour personality of a plate of halibut. Also, Mark Stein had already left for Chelsea, the board had used Stein's transfer cash to pay off the overdraft so Joe had no money to spend, and apart from being Scottish,

Joe showed little resemblance to Lou Macari.

What was it with Scottish managers? Before the recent era of foreign managers it was fashionable to have your very own Scottish manager. For example, Manchester United had Alex Ferguson, Blackburn had Kenny Dalglish, Liverpool had Graeme Souness (unfortunately for them), Rotherham United had Archie Gemmill (?!), and lucky old Dumbarton had Jim Fallon.

Who the hell is Jim Fallon?! Jim is 10th in The Guardian Top 10 Worst Managers, by virtue of losing 31 games out of 34, before astonishingly persuading the board to keep him on for another season! 13 games later they finally realised their mistake. Compared to him Joe Jordan was a management giant!

So what good things can we say about Joe? Didn't he re-sign Wayne Biggins? With goals in short supply, Biggins, who by now had bizarrely rejoined Macari at Celtic, was brought back to Stoke. However, Jordan's biggest coup was for the **1994/95** season, when he signed Paul Peschisolido from Karren Brady. Sorry, I mean from Birmingham City.

Surely the fans warmed to him then? Joe didn't give them a chance. After an opening day 1-0 win against Tranmere, things went considerably pear-shaped with four awful performances, culminating in two 0-4 defeats. With boardroom bust-ups seemingly every five minutes, and the team in the relegation zone, something had to give. After only five games, Joe supposedly jumped, although he later said he was pushed. "I never resigned, I was told to go. I would never have quit."

When my girlfriend first saw this picture of Joe Jordan she ran screaming from the room.

(© News Group Newspapers)

It's a good thing Joe hasn't written an autobiography of life behind the dream, giving his version of affairs!? In 2004 Joe published his autobiography *Behind The Dream*, giving his version of affairs.

Oh blimey. Go on then, what does he say? Well, firstly, he says that when Liam Brady left Celtic, Joe left too as he didn't want to stay on without Liam. He only stayed a further 24 hours to prepare the week's training schedule.

Does it really take 24 hours to do that?! For Joe it does, apparently. He then described his friend Lou as a shadowy companion for the time that Joe was at Stoke. He felt like he was keeping Lou's seat warm until the Celtic job went sour, concluding that he was in the wrong place at the wrong time.

Doesn't that sound familiar?! He says chairman Peter Coates was apologetic when he paid up Jordan's contract in order to bring back Macari, which makes it sound like "by mutual consent". Jordan had actually arranged the meeting to discuss buying players.

Two future Stoke City managers fight it out.

So Jordan wasn't that keen on leaving? He felt that he'd done reasonably well overall, and that the team had had an "average" start to the new season.

Reasonably well? That doesn't sound very convincing! This "average" start in fact found them playing dismally and lying in 22nd place. (Actually, that does sound kind of average, now you mention it.) However, even The Sentinel described it as a "poor start to the season" when he left.

Any other inconsistencies? He also says that the previous season saw Stoke finish close to the play-offs to the "old first division", when in fact it was the Premier League (and 10th isn't exactly close to the play-offs). He also implies that Lou was sacked after (or during) this "average" start, when he'd actually left Celtic three months before. In fact the lack of many actual dates and supporting information in his book makes it a frustrating read. Give me Alan Ball's book any time.

Is it that bad a book? He even fails to mention that his next club, Bristol City, knocked Stoke out of the FA Cup! You would have thought he'd have mentioned that! I mean, what sort of football book is this??

Where'd he go next? Back to Bristol City (which didn't work out), then briefly coached Northern Ireland with Lawrie McMenemy (which didn't work out), before joining Huddersfield supporting none other than Lou Macari (which didn't work out either). When that all fell apart, he got a call out of the blue from Harry Redknapp who got him coaching Portsmouth, where he has finally found his niche. I think they've just won the FA Cup. Can't be bad.

Has success finally gone to his head? I'm not even going to bother answering that.

Jordan: A smile for every occasion

No.13 – Asa Hartford

8ᵗʰ September – 29ᵗʰ September 1994 (caretaker manager)

Aha! Another Scottish manager?! Told you they were popular in the 80s & 90s. Yes, Asa had been Joe Jordan's assistant manager.

Great. So what does Joe Jordan say about working with Asa at Stoke in his autobiography? He fails to mention him at all.

Well, that's not very friendly. What do we know about him? Famous West Brom, Manchester City and Scotland player, best known for an aborted transfer to Leeds when they discovered he had a hole-in-the-heart. Went on to play in the World Cup, and score the winner for Norwich in the final of the Milk (League) Cup at Wembley.

Hartford in a white shirt just in case Leeds changed their minds

So, three weeks in charge. Did it go all wrong? Actually, he did well. He won three league games in a row in style, before announcing that he was ruling himself out as a candidate for the job. He then struggled to get past Third Division Fulham in the Coca-Cola cup (2-3 & 1-0, going through on away goals), and lost to Derby. However, he took over with the club in 22ⁿᵈ position and left with them in 8ᵗʰ spot in Division One.

But he didn't actually leave, did he? No, he hung around at Stoke as Macari's assistant before becoming coach at Manchester City for several years, firstly with Alan Ball and then Kevin Keagan. He's presently at Accrington Stanley.

Good story about Asa Hartford? Apparently (so how true it is we just don't know!), a Scottish radio station recently asked listeners to phone in and tell them where they were when Archie Gemmill scored that great dribbling goal against Holland in the 1978 World Cup finals. One said he had just returned from burying his mother, another said he watched the game at his wedding reception, but a third caller said: "I remember exactly where I was. I was 10 yards away screaming at the greedy wee b*stard to pass the ball!" It was Asa Hartford!

No.14 – Lou Macari (again!)

29ᵗʰ September 1994 – 1ˢᵗ July 1997 (although really it was April)

The prodigal son returns?! Hell, it didn't work out at Celtic, so why not.

What had gone wrong? He replaced Liam Brady, but didn't appear to do any better than him, ending the season 4ᵗʰ in the Scottish Premier, one place below Motherwell. Yes, Motherwell!

So he was ousted? There had been a takeover of the club in the spring, and the new regime eventually sacked him. One of their grumbles was that he hadn't moved his family up from Stoke, which caused concern at the club for some reason.

Why? Coz Celtic is in Glasgow, apparently, not Trentham (although my Sat-Nav reckons it's near Warrington). Anyway, their loss, our gain.

He started like before, I suppose, a bit sluggishly? A great 4-1 win against West Brom, was followed by a string of inconsistent results. This culminated in a 1-3 Christmas defeat by Joe Jordan's soon-to-be-relegated Bristol City.

Hey, you did want a signed copy, didn't you?

Well, at least that couldn't happen again! And then three weeks later it happened again. Jordan's Bristol City beat Stoke 1-3, this time knocking them out of the FA Cup, and this time at the Victoria Ground.

At least they didn't get knocked out of the cup by bottom side Notts County! And then they were knocked out of the Anglo-Italian Cup in the semi-finals by bottom club Notts County. A home defeat by Port Vale (0-1) was also hard to stomach. A small consolation in the Coca-Cola cup where Stoke went out with some dignity at Liverpool (1-2).

How bad did it look? Relegation began beckoning. But spirited wins against West Brom (3-1), Bristol City (2-1, sending them and Jordan down) and Millwall (4-3) left Stoke a flattering 11th to finish on.

What was the problem behind the scenes? The board had to decide whether to upgrade the Victoria Ground for the Taylor Report (all-seater stadiums) or build a new ground. The fans felt disenfranchised, and the board went for a new ground anyway, but they needed money to do this, which left Macari under-funded. Subsequently, attendances suffered, which meant less revenue etc.

Lou Macari being stalked by a disguised Chic Bates (right)

So next season, 1995/96, was a disaster?! Far from it. Mind you, it started pretty awfully with some dire results, including a 0-1 home defeat by Port Vale (again!). Soon Stoke were trawling along in last-but-one place for a few weeks. However, performances were generally good, and when they drew 0-0 with Chelsea in the Coca-Cola cup, results started coming. Stoke then beat Chelsea 1-0 in the second leg at Stamford Bridge, with Peschisolido the hero!

Was Peschisolido the new Mark Stein? Not really, but the Canadian played with flair. Soon after the Chelsea game, though, he lost his place in the first team. He was sold back to Birmingham in March, allegedly without Macari's knowledge.

So Macari didn't have a new Mark Stein? Not so. Macari got Mike Sheron in a suspiciously cheap exchange deal with Norwich in November.

Was this the famous deal where Macari off-loaded the hapless Keith Scott, who was actually valued more than Sheron on paper?! The story goes that Martin O'Neil was in the process of leaving Norwich at the time and allegedly acquired Scott as a parting "gift" to his chairman. (O'Neil wasn't so generous when his Leicester met Stoke in the playoffs a few months later.)

Was this Macari's best season? Yes. Sheron went on to score 15 goals in 23 games. Soon Stoke were in the top half, and pushing for promotion by February (in 3rd place) by beating high-flyers Ipswich, Leicester and Birmingham. However, they had a terrible March, including ANOTHER 0-1 defeat by Vale (that stupid 12 second Bogie goal), and despite a spirited recovery finished a credible 4th, and in the play-offs for the Premier League for the first time.

Obviously Stoke didn't win the play-offs? Bloody Leicester City. Stoke were all over them in the Filbert Street 0-0 clash, but were appalling in front of their own supporters, losing 0-1. Game over.

Still, tomorrow's another day, as the saying goes? A plethora of players left (Sandford, Overson, Gleghorn, Potter etc), many concerned about Stoke's finances over the new ground being built (and their own finances, I suppose!)

Giant-sized Lou Macari! (© Bob Bond 2006)
Lou was a good 50 yards from
Archie Gemmill when he scored
against Holland (ie. on the bench)

Any new blood?! Macari brought in Graham Kavanagh from Middlesbrough to steady the nerves in midfield. In came promising youngster Andy Griffin, and the Golden One, Mark Stein, returned on-loan. The new season, **1996-97**, started reasonably, but cracks started to show, mainly due to injuries. The season sagged in the middle, and the play-offs were never really a possibility. Stoke finished 12th. Their last emotional game at the Victoria Ground was another defeat of West Brom, by 2-1.

But did they beat Vale?! Soundly, by 2-0, with Mike Sheron on top form. He finished the season with 24 goals, which (worryingly) was 16 more than anyone else.

Was Sheron destined for the Premiership? No, he was destined for… QPR!? They paid £2.75m at the end of the season, by which time Macari was gone.

Gone?! Where did he go?! Officially he left to fight the long and drawn out lawsuit against Celtic. But with the club about to move ground to the Britannia Stadium, and with Sheron about to be sold to supposedly pay for it, Macari got the feeling he wasn't wanted anymore. After saying that he might have to leave, it appears that he was quickly shown the door. (He subsequently brought a lawsuit against Stoke.) Chic Bates and Mike Pejic effectively took over for the last few weeks.

I bet there'll be more about that in his book about his life in football? Yes, we've already plugged his *Football, My Life* book, thank you very much.

Was there a happy ending for Lou Macari? Sadly, no. He lost his case against Celtic in 1998. He appealed, but lost that as well. Although the judge found Macari to be "amiable" and Celtic's Fergus McCann to be "devious" and "arrogant", she ruled against Macari as he had failed to take orders (!) With the rising legal costs, Macari was hit by another tragedy, the suicide of his son in Trentham. He tried to restart his career managing Huddersfield with Joe Jordan in 2000, but although they were doing well, after a reshuffle in the boardroom they were out.

What is his legacy? He changed things at Stoke. So much so that we knew that there would be no more dumb managers, no more boardroom shenanigans, no more trouble from disgruntled fans. Order had been restored. And we had a new ground. The future, thanks mainly to Lou Macari, looked rosy! Thanks, Lou.

No.15 – Chic Bates (again!)

1ˢᵗ July 1997 – 22ⁿᵈ January 1998

Ah, the return of Stoke's best ever manager…(sort of)? He knew if he stalked Macari long enough, he'd get the job of his dreams.

What, Stoke manager?! No, caretaker manager of Celtic! When Macari left Glasgow, Chic stayed on a bit before rejoining Lou at Stoke. Then when the Stoke board failed to replace Macari with David Webb, Sammy McIlroy, Kevin Keagan, Chris Waddle, Denis Smith (now at Oxford), Joe Royle, Peter Beardsley (he was made an "incredible" offer to become player-coach!), Chris Nicholl, John Rudge (?), Paul Bracewell, Dave Watson and even Ron Atkinson…… Chic got the Stoke job. Poor sod.

Was it that bad? This was the unforgettable **1997/98** season. It was that bad. For starters, the new Britannia Stadium was chaos on match days, with queues everywhere, and yet loads of empty seats. The wind blew through the open corners, taking with it any atmosphere, but then the team weren't any good playing at their new home anyway. The fans got fed up of the match day farce, and started to give chairman Peter Coates more and more stick.

Good things to say here? Bates could only afford to buy one player, and he chose striker Peter Thorne, a shrewd long-term buy. Then after a couple of months he got help from Alan Durban who was brought back to help Chic out, as things got a bit ropey early on.

How ropey did things get? With Durban's help, Chic pulled the club away from the relegation zone. But despite reaching 6ᵗʰ with wins against Vale (2-1) and at Manchester City (1-0), Stoke started to nose dive around Halloween. By New Year they'd reached 15ᵗʰ

Chic Bates when he played alongside Tony Pulis

spot and got knocked out of the Coca-Cola cup 1-3 to Leeds and the FA Cup 1-3 to West Brom, teams they'd got used to beating. But worse was yet to come.

Was this where they lost 0-7 at home to Birmingham? Somehow The Sentinel had got hold of a list of players that the club wanted rid of. Morale – or what was left of it – collapsed. The team fell apart and the fans went mad. They'd moved to the new ground in good faith, only to find that everything (apparently) was a shambles.

But who notices the fans anyway? The following game (ironically against Bradford City) the Sky TV cameras were in and millions watched as supporters deliberately marched in late for the game protesting against Coates. The fans began to get mobilised, including boycotting Stoke facilities (catering, shop, tickets etc). Coates handed over chairmanship to his friend Keith Humphreys, but fans weren't fooled.

So was Chic sacrificed? If you mean was he burnt as an offering to the Gods, then no. If you mean was he demoted to coach till the end of the season, then you're right on the button. Stoke were 14th after beating Bradford 2-1.

Another nice guy bows out. Chic had battled hard, and hadn't really lost. He stayed on as he'd known Kamara from his time stalking Macari at Swindon Town. But he could at least have warned us as to what to expect!

STOKE CITY

No.16 – Chris Kamara

22ⁿᵈ January - 8ᵗʰ April 1998

Unbelievable!? You can say that again!

No, really!! Unbelievable!? Yes yes, I get the point. This is the star-of-Sky-Sports, Chris Kamara's one word catchphrase, I assume. But in those days he was a credible manager.

You've got to be kidding?!
No, honestly! He'd played circa 700 league games at clubs such as Stoke and Leeds, before retiring at Bradford City to be assistant manager. Not long after that they made him manager, and within months had turned a mid-table side into Wembley playoff winners. He soon established them as a mid-table 1ˢᵗ Division side.

And he gave them up for Stoke? Well, after they inexplicably sacked him, he did. However, he really believed that Stoke would soon be an established Premier League club, something he couldn't see for Bradford City.

T-shirt captures Chris in religious cult mood!!?
(Check out eBay)

But weren't Bradford promoted to the Premier the following year? Yeah, unbelievable! Who'd have backed them instead of Stoke, eh?! Well, not Kamara, obviously. He described his appointment at Stoke as "a gift from God". It certainly was from out of the blue.

So, how was he going to get Stoke into the Premier? Well, by firstly selling their best player, left back Andy Griffin, for £1.5m to Newcastle, where he did rather well. Then by fielding a bewildering set of players for the next 11 weeks

Chris and this haircut used to play at Swindon.
(© News Group Newspapers)

(to no avail). Even brought in veteran goalkeeper Neville Southall on loan from Everton. But Kamara failed to win over the players with his antics, even putting them all up for sale in a last bid to motivate them. After 10 games (5 defeats & 5 draws) Stoke had gone from 14th to bottom of the league. They then lost 1-5 at Oxford, 0-3 to Tranmere and 0-2 at bottom club Reading, before Kamara resigned.

Have you deliberately missed out his only win as Stoke manager? Oh yes, sorry. After the Oxford game, Stoke beat fellow strugglers QPR (with Mike Sheron) by 2-1, taking them briefly above Reading. It wasn't to last.

Anything else we should know about "Kammy"? Would you believe he was the first footballer in the English game to be convicted in court for on-the-field violence? Whilst with Macari's Swindon he apparently broke Shrewsbury's Jim Melrose cheekbone, catching him with his elbow. This was seen to be GBH, and he was fined £1200.

That world-famous Playstation game made world-famous by ... Chris Kamara?

He's not got an OBE then? No, but he is unique as the only Stoke manager with a Sony Playstation game named after him: *Chris Kamara's Street Soccer*. It got rave reviews.

In *Street Soccer*, does Chris rant at his players and put them all up for sale? Er, no, but you can play a team of Dutch women on Easter Island, although it doesn't explain anywhere why you'd want to do this.

A bit too obvious a name for his autobiography? *My Story, Unbelievable!*

No.17 – Alan Durban (again!)

8th April - 13th May 1998 (caretaker manager)

What had he been doing all season? He'd been brought in to assist Chic Bates originally, but curiously stayed on as a youth scout under Kamara. When Kamara left after 14 games, they dragged Durban out of the boot room (although technically scouts don't live in boot rooms).

Did he know what he had to do? He had five games to keep bottom club Stoke City FC in the 1st Division.

How did it go? Firstly, Stoke beat Alan Ball's Portsmouth, also fighting relegation, by 2-1. This was followed by defeat at Crewe (0-2). Many felt that the Crewe game was the decider, even though Stoke then beat Norwich 2-0 to climb out of the relegation zone.

Good thing they didn't have to then play a promotion seeker? Ironically it was 2nd place Sunderland – Durban's former club - who duly sliced them up (0-3).

Was there a good finale to the season? With luck, Stoke could send down either Portsmouth or better still Port Vale! But first they had to get a result, preferably a win, at home to Manchester City (one place below them, and desperate for a win themselves).

It didn't make any difference in the end, did it? The result turned out to be irrelevant in the end as both Portsmouth and Vale won, sending Stoke and Man City down anyway. But a full house (and millions on Sky TV) watched Stoke fall apart big style, losing 2-5. To cap it all there was crowd violence during and after the game.

You couldn't really blame Durban for all this, could you? No. The board blamed the fans, and the fans blamed the board.

Did Durban make a run for it whilst they were busy blaming each other? Yes, not being a total fool. This time he got away for good!

No.18 – Brian Little

13th May 1998 - 11th June 1999

Why was everyone so impressed with the arrival of Brian Little? After not being able to attract a name-manager for seemingly ages, it was quite a surprise for Stoke to land Brian Little. He'd brought Darlington back from the dead (or The Conference as it is better known), took Leicester back to the Premier via the play-offs, and won the Coca-Cola cup with Aston Villa in 1996.

Brian Little's book explained how to rub your chin in bewilderment

He was a bit of hero at Aston Villa, wasn't he? He only ever played for Villa in his 10 year career. He helped them back to the First Division, then won the League Cup with them twice, scoring the late-late winner in the 1977 final. However, he had to retire at the age of only 26.

How come? Curiously, he was having a medical at Villa's bitter rivals Birmingham City. He was due to sign for them when they discovered the knee injury that ended his career.

Lucky for Birmingham City that they spotted that in time? Yes, that was lucky.

What's Brian Little famous for now? He is – or at least was - the only currently working *English* manager to have won a major trophy - until Harry Redknapp won the FA Cup.

So, what could possibly go wrong having Little as Stoke's manager?! What Stoke (and probably Little himself) didn't realise was that his career had started to slide. When he'd left Darlington buoyant, they immediately got relegated. When he left Leicester buoyant, they immediately got relegated. But when he quit Villa, they were a lowly 15th and went on to win 9 of their last 11 games to finish 7th. The tide had turned for Brian Little.

Why didn't anyone listen? Mainly because Little started the **1998/99** season with 6 wins in a row. And apart from a couple of days in October, Stoke were top of the league till December.

When did people start noticing the wheels coming off the wagon? Losing in the FIRST round of the Worthington Cup to Macclesfield, getting knocked out of the FA Cup to Third Division Swansea, and going out of the AutoWindShield to Third Division Rochdale. So, no cup-run money to buy players with.

Well, more time to concentrate on the league, then? You would have thought, but with injuries stacking up, the points started drying up. December (4 defeats) and February (4 defeats) were particularly dire. Remember, this was the 2nd Division.

Did the Britannia Stadium feel any more at home? It might have done for away teams, but not for Stoke. Away form was actually better than home!

An unlikely T-shirt for wearing around Stoke-on-Trent

Couldn't Brian Little turn things around? He would declare a performance to be the worst he'd ever seen, only for a subsequent game to be more dreadful than the last. Team spirit drifted away. Little looked like a rabbit in the headlights – he just seemed to run out of ideas.

Well, at least the club wasn't running out of money to pay everyone! And then the club announced that they were running out of money…it was all this concentrating-on-the-league business.

So, no lucrative playoff with Manchester City then? Nope. Stoke finished 8th. I mention this here in case Brian Little is reading this so he knows where we finished. He seemed totally oblivious at the time.

So, did the fans lynch him? Of course not. They had fallen further out with the board, in particular chief executive, Jez Moxey. Their protests had become more and more creative, and harder and harder to ignore.

Brian Little in an England shirt. He only had one cap, coming on as sub against Wales for Mick Channon. (© News Group Newspapers)

How did he escape? He jumped ship citing personal reasons. He then said he wanted another shot at the big time, and cheekily joined West Brom! (Compensation was subsequently agreed.) He was then sacked a few months later with WBA on the brink of relegation (they stayed up without him).

How did The Sentinel see this? "Little is no stranger to controversial exits – leaving Leicester and popping up at Aston Villa shortly afterwards."

Famous for recently saying? "I genuinely feel my management has worked everywhere except West Brom" !

Did OK at…? Hull City and Tranmere Rovers.

Did not so OK at…? Wrexham in 2007/08. He took over in November 2007 (second from bottom of new Division Two), and led Wrexham out of the league completely (finishing bottom). They then offered him a new 2-year deal! Well, good luck to them.

No longer famous for? Being the only currently working Football League manager to have won a major trophy. Can't have everything, I suppose.

Brian Little…in a box!

No.19 – Gary Megson

14th July - 15th November 1999

14th July - 15th November 1999

Is this the turning point we've all been waiting for?! That's the positive spin you've put on it. This was the real low point for the club. Stoke had been in the 2nd Division before, but now looked like they were staying for a long time. The club was in turmoil, with the supporters and the board at each other's throats over just about everything; the club having moved to a ground they didn't really own, but were still in financial peril; they'd just lost a supposedly decent manager, who could do nothing for them; even Tony Pulis turned down the manager's job, preferring to go to Bristol City (?!).

So, at their lowest point, they hired Gary Megson? I'm sure he'll be happy to hear it put like that. However, arguably he started the comeback that ultimately led to the Premier League.

Aren't there two schools of thought on his stay at Stoke? Some feel he was a lost opportunity with great potential, others see him as a dead loss and a relegation-monkey.

So which was he? Oh for argument's sake, we'll say he was both. He's been relegated with Norwich, WBA and Nottingham Forest. But he's done well at Stockport, West Brom (two promotions) and Bolton.

Someone, who clearly didn't like Megson, used to scribble all over his photographs

What else should we know? At Norwich he was called The General. He's a fiery, no nonsense character. But more importantly he had briefly been Chris Kamara's assistant at Bradford City! I'm not sure who's more embarrassed about that.

How did Stoke come by him? He fell out with 1st Division Stockport's chairman. Stoke snapped him up on a two year contract, whilst also hiring recently sacked Port Vale manager, John Rudge as "Director Of Football", a stupendously meaningless title.

How was that going to work? Apart from scouting, which he excelled at, Rudge's role seemed to be to work behind the scenes to stop the club from slipping on banana skins every five minutes.

Who keeps scribbling all over Gary Megson?!?

Did it work on the field? After 3 defeats in 4 games at the start of the **1999/2000** season, suddenly Thorne and Kavanagh came on tap. Megson peaked with a great run in October, taking Stoke to 3rd place, but blotted his copybook by losing 0-2 to his former club Blackpool in the FA Cup.

He didn't get sacked for that, did he? God, no. Suddenly, out of the blue, the club was taken over by an Icelandic consortium. They wanted a manager with an unpronounceable name, so Megson was made an offer he couldn't refuse. Stoke were 7th at the time.

Sentinel headline? "Megson Iced Out!" Megson apparently learnt his fate just before his last game, a 1-1 draw with Tony Pulis's Bristol City.

Did it bother him? Doubt it. Megson soon walked into West Bromwich Albion, who'd just sacked Brian Little, and had an exciting 4½ years there. Now manages Bolton in the Premier League. (Stoke play them in their first game!)

Unlikely parting comment on Megson from new Icelandic chairman?
"He'll never get anywhere with a name like that."

No.20 – Gudjon Thordarson

15th November 1999 - 15th May 2002

Was it about this time that Stoke City entered...THE TWILIGHT ZONE?!?! If you mean Stoke falling under the influence of Iceland and its dark winters illuminated by the kaleidoscopic Aurora Borealis, then yes. However, if you mean the club getting sucked into a strange parallel universe...then yes, I suppose that's also true!

How did The Potters end up in a parallel universe? It was actually Lou Macari's fault, as he'd signed Icelanders Toddy Orlygsson and Larus Sigurdsson. This attracted the attention of Gudjon Thordarson, then Iceland's most successful national coach. (He made never-qualifying-for-anything look impressive by almost qualifying for Euro 2000.) Gudjon saw potential for the club, and liaised with an Icelandic consortium who bought a majority holding from Peter Coates.

So what was different about this parallel universe? Well, for starters the club started to consult supporters, which initially confused fans as they found themselves without their main point of reference (ie. a club that didn't listen). The club also began to take a hard-line against the hooligan element, which was a welcome surprise. Then Gudjon's team started playing flowing attacking football, causing more bewilderment from fans. But most importantly Gudjon started signing players whose names no one could pronounce, which sent all reason out the window.

Gudjon enjoying a holiday in Wales

But now that Scottish managers were becoming a thing of the past, surely foreign managers and players were the norm? Well, yes, there was Arsène Wenger, Sven-Goran Eriksson, Mark Hughes (*Mark Hughes*??!). But this was 2nd Division Stoke City.

I think you're exaggerating these foreign names! OK, what about Brynjar Gunnarsson, Arnar Gunnlaugsson, Mikael Hansson, Bjarni Gudjonsson, Tony

Dorigo, Rikki Dadason, Frode Kippe, Stafan Thordarson, Henrik Risom, Birkir Kristinsson, Sergei Schtaniuk…

Hang about, Tony Dorigo doesn't count! You get the picture.

But could they play? Gudjon won his important first game 4-0 away to mid-table Wycombe. But despite great football, an improving home record at the Britannia, and beating top clubs such as Preston (2-1) and Wigan (2-1), results were never quite good enough to break into the promotion spots. They even lagged behind the playoff places.

That doesn't sound like a parallel universe. That was normal, wasn't it? But then Port Vale got relegated, and Stoke got to Wembley in the AutoWindShield.

Another Stoke Wembley victory? Absolutely, a 2-1 win over Bristol City. Kavanagh scored first with Peter Thorne scoring the winner, sliding home a deflected cross from close range with 9 minutes left.

Even in his youth, Gudjon had a penchant for ill-fitting tracksuits

Stein, Sheron, and now Thorne … another great Stoke goalscorer? Definitely. It was the Thorne and Kavanagh show, although puppet master Thordarson's new system made them play.

But it didn't mean promotion? It took six wins on the trot just to get above Bristol Rovers into a playoff spot before the last game of the season. Stoke then lost their last game at mid-table Reading. Thankfully, Rovers lost at already relegated Cardiff City! Phew.

So Stoke were on a roll as they went into the playoffs? Despite winning 3-2 at home, the away leg at Gillingham was a fiasco. Thorne was out injured, Clarke and Kavanagh were sent off needlessly, and despite making it to extra-time, the nine remaining men were beaten 0-3.

There's always another season! But the new board were insistent that **2000/01** was promotion season. Fans were quite insistent too. But then it all went a bit wonky.

Wonky?! In what way? With initial injuries and fitness doubts, such as Peter Thorne, Thordarson's flowing attacking system stopped flowing. Despite criticism, Thordarson persisted with his dysfunctional system, and eventually, with the return of Thorne, Stoke slowly climbed the league. But confidence was hit, and Thordarson started to struggle to keep the squad together. As discontent spread, so did transfer requests.

Good thing Stoke didn't then lose in the FA Cup to one of those embarrassing non-league teams! And then they lost in the FA Cup to one of those embarrassing non-league teams, Nuneaton Borough (0-1).

Well, er, a good run in the Worthington League Cup would make up for this! It would have done, if Stoke hadn't then lost 0-8 at home to Liverpool, a mere 8 days after the Nuneaton game.

But the AutoWindShield…?! Lost in the Semi-final by a golden goal to Port Vale! The game had even been moved to the Britannia.

Ouch! Did it all fall apart? It should have done, but this was a parallel universe. Heroically, Thordarson held things together. He still trod on people's shoes, and he may not have been the best-dressed track-suit manager, but he strung along enough results to keep Stoke in the play-offs for the whole of the second half of the season, winning their last three games just to be sure.

So Stoke were on a roll as they went into the playoffs? And just like last time, it was a fiasco. 0-0 at home, then a 2-4 defeat at Walsall. There was only one red card for Stoke this time, and Thorne at least came on as a substitute.

But they gave Gudjon another chance? Well, they'd given Mick Mills several chances, so why should Gudjon be any different. However, he daringly and openly staked his reputation on promotion. He cut his own contract down from three years to just one.

Did promotion look likely? Definitely not. Several players left, including Kavanagh to Cardiff for £1m and Thorne (reluctantly) for £1.7m. The money stabilised the club, but did little for Gudjon. Then there were a string of bizarre injuries. Then Gudjon fell out with the press. Then…

So how did the increasingly dishevelled-looking Thordarson snatch triumph from the jaws of seeming disaster in 2001/02? As this was a parallel universe, Stoke won 8 out of 10 games after Thorne left. After beating Wycombe 5-1 in December, Stoke went top, and were top 5 for the rest of the season. They were more than a match for top clubs Reading (2-0) and Brighton (3-1), but it was playoffs again.

So Stoke were on a roll as they went into the playoffs? Don't keep saying that!! In fact it was Cardiff (with Kavanagh and Thorne) who were the in-form side, proving it by beating Stoke 1-2 at the Britannia.

So that was the end of Thordarson? Absolutely. He was sacked a couple of weeks later.

Hang on, aren't we missing something out? Staggeringly, O'Connor equalised in the last seconds of the 2nd leg at Cardiff. Then late in extra time his free-kick was deflected in off the bum of someone called Souleyman Oulare. Stoke were through to the play-off final!

Souleyman Oulare?!? You're making him up? Apparently he was Belgian Footballer Of The Year in 1999. But soon after Thordarson signed him, and making one substitute appearance, he developed DVT (a blood clot). When he recovered, he only played this one other game for Stoke, coming on as substitute in the 70th minute. He didn't even play in the final at the Millennium Stadium, where Brentford were seen off by 2-0, and so he went back to Belgium.

So that was the end of Thordarson? Absolutely. Four days later, the board sacked him.

How come? Effectively for not always appreciating the club's financial constraints. Sounds like most managers, that.

Where did he go? Barnsley then Notts County, both with little success. But is now back on top in Iceland club management.

Not to be confused with…? Er, there was no one you could ever confuse Gudjon Thordarson with.

No.21 – Steve Cotterill

27th May - 10th October 2002

Tell us the weird and wonderful story of Steve Cotterill? Well, as Stoke were still in the Icelandic Twilight Zone, this story won't make much sense either.

Is it true he only played 73 league games in his 8 years as a professional footballer? Yes, but as a tall centre forward he scored 25 goals in that time. He had been at Premier League Wimbledon for 4 years, but only made 25 appearances. He then joined Bournemouth, where he became a firm favourite with supporters, before a knee injury finished his career. And who had signed him? A guy called Tony Pulis.

So, he was Tony Pulis's protégé? Not only that, but both Pulis and Cotterill (and Steve Coppell) were short-listed for the Stoke job. But it was Cotterill that got the three year contract. I'm surprised he could see that far ahead!

Why on earth did Stoke want him? At the age of only 37 he was seen as the boy-wonder at the time, as he'd taken Cheltenham Town from the Southern League Division Six to the Football League 2nd Division in 5 years.

The vacant look, the empty terraces, and Lawrie Sanchez? It could only be Wimbledon.

So what? Brian Little had done that with Darlington. Yes, we should have spotted the similarities. In many ways Cotterill was "son-of-Brian-Little": in that, he knew what he was getting into, but didn't stay long enough to face the consequences.

Anything to say in his defence? At the start of the **2002/03** season, with Stoke now back in the 1st Division, he brought harmony and fitness back to the dressing room, but only 3 victories in his 13 games in charge. Also lost to 3rd

Division Bury in the League Cup. Signed Greenacre (immediately injured) and Mooney (immediately suspended). Had the fewest yellow cards in the league.

Take a good look at this man – as he will soon disappear!

Did he then sneak off and join West Brom? Certainly not. He then sneaked off and joined Sunderland like Alan Durban had 20 years before, except he became assistant manager to Howard Wilkinson. They finished bottom of the Premier League with only 19 points, and they both got sacked, which proved that it wasn't the brightest idea.

What did he say about Stoke supporters when he left? He said, "I haven't a single bad word to say about them."

And what did Stoke supporters say about him when he left? Go on, have a guess!

And what did Sunderland's chairman say? He said he was amazed that Stoke had insisted on a clause in Cotterill's contract that allowed such a small amount of compensation to be paid if he left (or was sacked).

And what did the Stoke board subsequently say? It wasn't small (£165k), AND we want £1m for an illegal approach.

So is Cotterill now sweeping the streets? Certainly not. He was at Burnley for 3 years, although they never finished above Stoke. Rumoured to be working with England's Under-21s.

His nickname? "Quitterill". Hardly seems fair…oh, I don't know though.

Where'd he go?!?

No.22 – Dave Kevan

10th October – 1st November 2002 (caretaker manager)

Dropped in at the deep end? Definitely. Stoke lost all four games under Dave. Goals-for 2, goals-against 10. Equally as bad a record as Tony Lacey (qv). Wolves (0-2), Sheff Utd (1-2), Rotherham (0-4), and Watford (1-2).

Couldn't we have got Asa Hartford back as caretaker? Sorry, he was busy at Manchester City.

In fairness,...? In fairness, all four games were against top sides.

Didn't Alan Ball sign him originally in 1990? Aha, now you remember him. You're not going to blame it all on Alan Ball, are you? He made his debut against Vale, won an Autoglass Trophy medal, but after Tony Pulis signed him for Bournemouth an injury caused him to quit at only 27 – just like Steve Cotterill! He returned to Stoke as Youth team coach in 1998, becoming first team coach in 2001 under Thordarson.

Another good guy? Despite the four defeats, generally felt to be a Stoke hero and a nice guy.

When Dave grew up he would manage Stoke City

What happened to Dave Kevan? He stayed on as coach under Tony Pulis, but then teamed up with Steve Cotterill as his assistant manager when Steve went to Burnley in 2004. Stayed 3 years before becoming assistant manager at Notts County, keeping them away from relegation to The Conference.

Dave all grown up

Could Cotterill do without Kevan? As it turns out, no. Ten days after Kevan left, Cotterill had a mutual-consent split with Burnley.

What did Steve Cotterill say about him? "Dave is probably a different character to myself. He is a really good, honest citizen and a popular character."! However, I'm not sure he meant to say it quite like that.

No.23 – Tony Pulis

1st November 2002 - 28th June 2005

He didn't look like The Messiah? They never do.

Was he an obvious choice? Certainly not. He didn't have an OBE or an MBE, he hadn't won the World Cup, or scored the winner in the FA Cup Final or the League Cup Final, he hadn't won the League Championship, he hadn't played against Brazil, or been England Captain, or won the Fourth Division Championship, or had a hole in his heart…frankly, I don't know why he applied at all.

*Tony enjoying a joke
with his team-mates*

Particularly as he'd been offered the job before…? Oh yes, he was first choice when Brian Little left in 1999, but Pulis went to Bristol City as he felt they had more "ambition".

What did he mean by that?! Probably that Bristol City didn't have all the problems that Stoke had at the time (debts, hooligans, mass-protests, managers' graveyard, etc). Now the club had sorted out a lot of these problems, AND they were back in the 1st Division.

But this time he wasn't first choice? As Ipswich had just sacked George Burley, the board invited George to watch Stoke. However, he took one look (home defeat against Watford) and thought better of it. But not before the club had called a press-conference to announce him as manager. George later said it was because he only wanted a contract till the end of the season. He now manages Scotland, which HE thinks is a better job!

So Tony Pulis was appointed? Pulis had been interviewed when Cotterill had got the job, but only became available again 2 days before he was appointed, after a generous settlement from Portsmouth. Boy, did he come with baggage.

What, a suitcase full of tracksuits and baseball caps? Very funny. No, a controversial history. He'd been a tenacious defender/midfielder with Bristol Rovers and Bournemouth, although he'd also played for a club called Happy Valley! (It's in Hong Kong.) He became assistant to Harry Redknapp at

Bournemouth, succeeding him as manager. He had most success at Gillingham (promotion), until he was sacked after losing the play-off final to Manchester City. He received compensation from them after a bitter court case, and later some from Portsmouth, who also sacked him after he'd saved them from relegation. There's gratitude for you.

How did he get on at the "ambitious" Bristol City? The fans were on his back from day one because he'd played for Bristol Rovers. So putting up with any stick at Stoke was a doddle in comparison.

Any other problems? He has been accused of playing negative "direct football" (ie. the long-ball game, a sort of kick-and-run), and for signing big guys who play rough and get loads of red cards. It was also said that he lacked any charisma, which really was harsh.

So after two years out from management, didn't he find it difficult being back in the hot seat? Although he'd been sacked a couple of times, he'd never been relegated, and he was determined to keep it that way. So he played the Waddington/Durban/Macari card: start by shoring up the defence and stop conceding so many goals.

Did it work? Nope. But then it was always going to take time, which unlike his predecessors, he didn't have very much of. Stoke lost their first four games under Pulis, making it 8 in a row. It took 10 games under Pulis to get a win, and that was against bottom side Sheffield Wednesday (3-2).

How does it compare to Kamara's 14 games in charge? Very similar, in fact, although Pulis managed two wins to Kamara's one. However, whilst still bobbling around the relegation area, they then lost 0-6 at Nottingham Forest and sank to the bottom themselves. They did then reach the 5th round of the FA Cup, only then losing to Chelsea by 0-2.

Doesn't sound like a shored up defence to me! Ah, but then Pulis brought in Mark Crossley on loan from Middlesbrough (using the Chelsea windfall money). With Crossley in goal Stoke only lost two out of 12, only conceded seven goals, and won five of their last 8 games. On the final day they needed a point against Reading to stay up, but a goal by on-loan Akinbiyi gave them all three and secured 1st Division football.

But they were still favourites to go down in 2003/04? But with several new signings, including Gifton Noel-Williams from Watford, Stoke bucked the trend and started strongly with three wins, although one was against Rochdale (League Cup).

They didn't get knocked out of the League Cup by Pulis' former club Gillingham, did they? Then they got knocked out of the League Cup by Pulis's former club Gillingham (0-2). This led to a poor run of results, culminating in December with Pulis's beloved Cardiff City doing the double over Stoke, sending them into the relegation zone.

So the pundits were right afterall? Not so fast. 7 wins in 10 over Christmas/New Year sent them back to chasing the play-offs, and now Stoke were beating a lot of the top sides (for a change!) like Nottingham Forest (2-1), Sunderland (3-1), West Ham (1-0), promoted West Brom (4-1) … and Rochdale (League Cup) (!).

Tony Pulis at Bristol Rovers where he played alongside Chic Bates and Alan Ball

But did they get revenge on Gillingham? Almost. Gillingham needed a point to stay up in the last game of the season at the Britannia Stadium. As the referee didn't see Carl Asaba's late header crossing the Gillingham goal-line, the game ended 0-0. Stoke finished a respectable 11th.

What was it that the crazed Gillingham chairman wrote in a programme about Tony Pulis, according to Stephen Foster's brilliant "*She Stood There Laughing*"? Was it "He was the most evil, vindictive and malicious person I have ever met."?

Well, that's not very nice: we don't like him at all if he says things like that! Can we use that quote?! Better not. Let's just say they didn't get on.

Pity we didn't beat Gillingham then. We did the following **2004/05** season (2-0), and yes Gillingham were relegated after failing to win their last game – Crewe did win and stayed up.

And where were all these Vale players coming from? Hm. First it was Lee Mills, then Dave Brammer, then Steve Guppy. Who next? Martin bleedin Foyle? John Rudge was pushing it a bit here.

But the season went well? A good start got better when they beat Ipswich in a 3-2 thriller to go top after only 8 games. Then the Icelandic board made a crucial mistake of offering Pulis £2m to strengthen the squad for promotion, … and the team subsequently nose-dived.

Could he buy whom he wanted, or did they have to have foreign names?
There was a healthy exchange of views on this matter (!) Pulis was
painstakingly negotiating a new contract, and seemed less inclined to search
abroad for players, as he had his own UK contacts. In the end, both sides had
to settle for a draw, but more Icelandic players arrived all the same.

What was the result? 1-0, mainly. In the 17 league games between October
and February, 15 of them had a 1-0 scoreline (7 of them wins), and 2 had a 0-0
scoreline. Supporters were starting to become vocal on the dull negative long-
ball football, describing it as The Binary System (1-0, 0-0, 0-1).

But table position was a roller-coaster? After going top, Stoke had seven
games without a win (14th), then just before Christmas they revived to go 6th,
but afterwards lost six in a row (although one was a credible 1-2 to Arsenal in
the FA Cup) (16th). A pre-Easter revival (5 wins in 6)
saw Stoke chasing a playoff spot, before self-destructing
(7 defeats in 10) back to mid-table, finishing 12th.

Not more boring statistics?? They scored only 36 goals
– only Rotherham (bottom by a mile) scored less (35).
They conceded only 38 goals, only Wigan (promoted)
conceded less (35). Strangely, average attendances were
the highest since Lou Macari's promotion season. Obviously after looking
through these fabulously presented statistics, the Icelandic board put the club
up for sale. They felt they'd spent enough to be a Premier team by now, …only
they weren't there. Some certainly felt that Pulis had spent enough of their
money.

So after negotiating a new contract, he suddenly got sacked? He'd fallen
out with the Icelandic board for the last time, particularly over exploiting the
foreign market.

Any other reason? Rumour had it that the board thought that Peter Coates
would buy them out, and he favoured Pulis, who thus got his new contract.
When Coates' modest offer came in, the board weren't impressed, and so
didn't need Pulis anymore. So they decided on one last roll of the dice, with
another manager.

Many fans weren't sad to see Pulis go? True, but most of them later admitted
to being wrong about him. (I wonder why!)

What sort of things did they say? They said, "He's not the Messiah, he's a
very naughty boy!"

No.24 – Johan Boskamp

28th June 2005 – 23rd May 2006

Let me guess: Tony Pulis bought him to play for Bournemouth, and he then had a career-ending injury soon after?!!? Does it seem likely that Pulis would sign Dutchman Johan Boskamp?

Not unless he played for Bristol Rovers, Gillingham or Burnley. So who did he play for? The mighty Feyenoord, although he only played about 100 times for them in 10 years. But became a regular in the Belgian side "RWD Molenbeek", who won the league as soon as Johan joined (it is their only ever major trophy!). By the way, RWD stands for *Racing White Daring*! Honestly.

Where was he when Archie Gemmill scored against Holland in 1978? Aha! Good question. He was about 20 yards away, probably marking Asa Hartford! He only played a couple of times for Holland, but that game was one of them, coming on as substitute after 10 minutes for Neeskens.

Boskamp was a light, nimble centre forward

And that entitled him to manage Anderlecht? He managed several Belgian sides before and after Anderlecht, with some success. But for some reason he suddenly wanted to see the world, managing in Georgia, The United Arab Emirate, and Kuwait.

And he suddenly thought, I must give all this up to manage Stoke? Doesn't everybody?! Stoke's style of play was subsequently very different for the **2005/06** season. Although more attractive, it was very hit-or-miss, with red cards everywhere and results all over the place. The team were also doing better away from home again.

At least they didn't get beat by a non-league team in the FA Cup! Aha! Not this time. But they almost got beat by a non-league team, only seeing off Tamworth on penalties after a replay.

Isn't Boskamp best remembered for a punch-up with John Rudge?! No, he's not, but they did fall out.

What happened? Boskamp claimed he was undermined when Rudge supposedly tried to issue instructions to players via Boskamp's assistant Jan de Koning during a game at Coventry City that November. Boskamp's wanted them both sacked, or he would leave. As a compromise, both were sent on gardening leave for several months, but the story continued to run, fuelled by Boskamp. Eventually, de Koning was laid off.

But did the team look like getting promotion? They clawed their way back up to 5th position just before Christmas, but after Christmas was appalling, with 9 games without a win and then only 5 wins in the 22 remaining games. Stoke were lucky to finish 13th, one place lower than Pulis managed the year before.

Did he storm off in a huff? Certainly not. The club offered him a one-year deal, but he wanted two, so he left for Standard Liege. He lasted there only a few weeks. Now managing his eighth Belgian club.

Jan Boskamp was born so long ago he was in black and white

No.25 – Tony Pulis (again!)

15ᵗʰ June 2006 - ....

Were Stoke finally leaving the Twilight Zone? The Icelanders had had enough. So when Peter Coates turned up with a bucket full of cash, they grabbed it and scarpered. Then it was business as usual.

Did Coates really pay the reported £1.7m to buy back the club he had sold for £3.5m? Well, he had to sink millions more in to pay off the Icelandic loans and debts with the club. The Icelanders were also on a bonus if Stoke made the Premier League (just hedging their bets).

A Soviet spy satellite snapped this rare photo of a very young Tony Pulis. Around this time he apparently knew John Rudge briefly, before the latter was transferred to Bournemouth.

Why did Coates suddenly have all this money? It's his daughter's fault. Denise Coates persuaded her dad to move his betting shop business on to the internet (bet365), and before you could say "Jimmy Robertson", he was in the Top 30 richest people.

What?! Stoke's success is built on *gambling*?? I know, it's disgraceful. We should all gnash our teeth and repent.

And to make up for his sins, did he bring back one of Stoke's most popular managers to win over the fans? No, his first move was to wrestle Tony Pulis away from Plymouth. It took some doing. For some reason Plymouth didn't want to lose him, and Pulis was "happy" there. Bizarre. I mean, what does Plymouth have that Stoke doesn't?

Who would have thought that Stoke would end up with Coates and Pulis? You could'ner make it up, could you? Neither had been particularly popular in their previous stints at the club, so they really were the-pair-least-likely-to-succeed. Supporters ranged from sceptical to downright appalled, believing it would all end in tears. To them it was surely going to be "long-ball on a shoestring".

They had a lot of nerve showing their faces round here? Pulis reckoned that if Coates had the strength to come back, then so had he, particularly as Coates promised a reasonable budget, instead of a "bottom-three" budget that Pulis had complained of in his first stint at Stoke.

Did he buy anybody good? Striker Ricardo Fuller from Southampton. The nod came from Pulis's former colleague Harry Redknapp, who'd signed Fuller twice. Then Pulis got Lee Hendrie on loan from Villa, and defender Andy Griffin back on loan from Portsmouth (Harry Redknapp again!).

Did they make any difference? You can bet your boots! The **2006/07** season started badly with one win in 10, plus a home defeat by Division Two's Darlington in the League Cup. As you can imagine, there were a lot of "told-you-so's" in the crowd.

Doesn't sound like they made any difference! That was before Fuller and Hendrie were brought in. Stoke then beat Leeds away (4-0) and Norwich (5-0). The wins kept coming – 5 in a row in November, and soon after Stoke were 4th. But following Christmas, the results stopped flowing, sunk by a steady stream of conceded late goals. February was typically dismal, although they did win 2-0 at top side Derby County and draw 2-2 at Roy Keane's soaring Sunderland.

Did they have a late surge? 4 wins and 2 draws left them 7th with one game left. All they had to do was win better than Southampton did in order to reach the playoffs.

Tony Pulis putting a brave face on a dreadful new shirt design.

And did they? Nope. Against QPR they conceded an early goal, had a goal disallowed, played against 10 men for the last 20 minutes, and only equalised in the 84th minute. They finished 8th.

So they sacked him and got Harry Redknapp in? We're not in the Twilight Zone now. This is real life. This is now the **2007/08** season!

In the film version will Tony Pulis be played by Leonardo DiCaprio, and Peter Coates by Morgan Freeman? Er, let's move on, shall we.

Was it a breeze from the start? Well, the on-loan Hendrie and Griffin signed for other clubs, and Danny Higginbotham went to Sunderland for £2.5m. However, Pulis found defender Ryan Shawcross (from Manchester United!) and striker Richard Cresswell (free from Leeds), both equally good at scoring.

I bet they got beat in the League Cup! Then they went out of the League Cup to Rochdale on penalties. But by mid-October they had only lost once in the league. A poor November was followed by a 12 match unbeaten run taking them back into the playoffs. They even beat West Brom (again!) 3-1 with a Ricardo Fuller hat-trick.

I bet they got beat in the FA Cup! Although almost toppling Newcastle United (0-0), they were crushed 1-4 in the replay, the day Kevin Keagan returned to the club.

I bet that must have broken their spirits. It sure did: Newcastle struggled for the rest of the season!

No, I meant it must have broken Stoke's spirits! Nope, quite the opposite. Five straight wins later, and Stoke were top of the league.

And then I bet they went through their typical shaky February/March period? Yes, one win in 8 games which left them…Hang on, they were still 2nd?! Hey? What's going on?

That's not right, surely. It seemed that the other top teams, particularly Watford and Bristol City, had also had a bad month. Shame on them.

So everything to play for? After losing at home 1-2 to late challengers Crystal Palace, there were four games left. Winning all four might not be enough. But they started by winning at Coventry 2-1, with Liam Lawrence putting on his shirt after 66 minutes, and taking it off again 12 minutes later.

He'll catch a chill, you mark my words. What was he playing at? He came on as substitute and ripped off his shirt after scoring, doing a convincing Incredible Hulk impression as he ran over to the fans.

What about the 6 pointer against Bristol City? Two first half Sidebe goals finished Bristol's promotion dreams in a cracking 2-1 win in front of the cameras.

The easiest of the four? Well, it should have been away to relegated Colchester. However, Cresswell's first half winner in a 1-0 win was almost overturned in the final seconds by a disallowed goal. Phew! Promotion would have been ours if Hull hadn't scored late in their game at Crystal Palace.

So, it went to the last game? Stoke now only needed a draw at home to relegation-threatened Leicester. This time results in the other games went Stoke's way (challenging Hull lost at Ipswich) not Leicester's (Southampton ending up winning). The goalless draw meant relegation for Leicester to the third tier for the first time in their history.

What about Stoke? PROMOTION TO THE PREMIER LEAGUE!!!
…for the first time in their history.

How will this affect Tony Pulis? Every week when he's interviewed on TV he'll have to blame the referee, claim there's a conspiracy against the club, accuse Drogba of diving, and threaten another manager. And he'll have to do this whilst wearing a suit and speaking in broken English in a foreign accent (as he's Welsh, that will just have to do).

Really? No. He won't change. Stubborn to the last, just how we like him. He's going to lead Stoke City in the Premier League the way that HE wants to, and that *will* be worth watching. I can't wait.

How did you know he would turn out alright? Because when he joined Stoke on 1st November 2002, he said the following, "*It doesn't matter to me whether I am 2nd, 3rd or 10th choice. What matters is I want to come here, and this is what I call a proper football club. Others might say it's a difficult job and not a good career move, but I don't look at it like that at all. It's a fantastic job. I am proud to be the manager.*" Brings a tear to your eye.

So we've finished now, have we? Yep, all 25 post-Waddington managers (according to the Stoke City official website); done and dusted.

Down the pub? Is the Pope a Catholic? Do bears poop in the woods? Are Stoke in the Premier League?

Er, yes. Then lead the way!

League positions, 1960-2008

Year	Division 1	Division 2	Division 3	Div 4
1960/1, 1961/2, 1962/3		18th, 8th, 1st		
1963/4, 1964/5, 1965/6, 1966/7, 1967/8, 1968/9, 1969/70, 1970/1, 1971/2, 1972/3, 1973/4, 1974/5, 1975/6, 1976/7	17th, 11th, 10th, 12th, 18th, 19th, 9th, 13th, 17th, 15th, 5th, 5th, 12th, 21th			
1977/8, 1978/9		7th, 3rd		
1979/80, 1980/1, 1981/2, 1982/3, 1983/4, 1984/5	18th, 11th, 18th, 13th, 18th, 22th			
1985/6, 1986/7, 1987/8, 1988/9, 1989/90		10th, 8th, 11th, 13th, 24th		
1990/1, 1991/2			14th, 4th	
Year	Premier	1st Division	2nd Division	3rd Div
1992/93			1st	
1993/4, 1994/5, 1995/6, 1996/7, 1997/8		10th, 11th, 4th, 12th, 23th		
1998/9, 1999/00, 2000/1, 2001/2			8th, 6th, 5th, 5th	
2002/3, 2003/4		21th, 11th		
Year	Premier	Championship	League 1	Lge 2
2004/5, 2005/6, 2006/7, 2007/8		12th, 13th, 8th, 2nd		*Port Vale!*

Acknowledgements

Where possible, permission for reproducing material has been sought, and we thank the many generous people and organisations who have allowed us to use this material (including Bob Bond, Philip Neill & Becci Fell). Apologies to any organisation that we've missed or we were just unable to trace. Furthermore, we have striven to ensure that all is factual, and hope that you agree that we have been fair in our appraisal

Thanks to Martin Poole, Little Al, Big Al, Steve & the rest. For Shell, Ad, Bek & Dyl.

A3